AREN'T WE
THE LUCKY ONES

A Story of Acceptance
For Those of Us Who Understand
That There Is No Free Will

- Secretary Michael

AREN'T WE THE LUCKY ONES
by Secretary Michael

3rd Revision
ISBN (print edition): 978-1-888712-14-8
ISBN (digital edition): 978-1-888712-03-2

✿

Machinists Union Press
web: www.machinistsunion.org
email: twimfina@gmail.com

To my fellow determinists:
May you find purpose
May you find direction
May you bring us with you

Contents

Aren't We the Lucky Ones

Purpose 7

CHAPTERS:

1. Valedictorian 8
2. Roommates 11
3. Waitress 14
4. Coach... 17
5. Secretary 19
6. My Classmates 21
7. The First Class 23
8. The Last Class.. 25
9. No Music Please 28
10. Class Cancelled 30
11. First Meeting at Una's 34
12. Escape to the Fountain Room 37
13. Pajama Circle for the Emma Darwinians.......... 41
14. Corky Comes 45
15. Hat Contest 47
16. Lasagna.. 55
17. Twimfina 60
18. Machinists Union Meets in the Library........... 64
19. B.B.Brice - Beans & Rice 67
20. Our Professor 73
21. Enemia... 75
22. Changing People Without Violence 81
23. Testosterone Theater Fountain-Flush............. 85
24. New Kitchen 93
25. Money 96
26. Doofus Gunshop Fountain-Flush................... 107
27. The Women Meet..114
28. Flophouse Dreams 129
29. Badluck Jail Fountain-Flush 127
30. Everyday Machinists 133
31. Lauterkeit 137

32. Things Could Have Been Different 141
33. Monkey See.. 144
34. Topsy Turvy 150
35. Thanksgiving... 154

Afterword 159

APPENDIX:

Genocide Slide 160
B.B.Brice Recipes... 164
Index of Concepts 170

Purpose

When I was in my late teens or early twenties, I came to the horrifying realization that a "free will" does not exist. Oh sure it *seems* like we have a free will - just like it *seems* that the sun revolves around the earth. But simple mechanics says otherwise.

Coming to this understanding back at that young age was paralyzing. To make matters worse, I had nobody I could talk with about it. And even if I had, I probably wouldn't have had the words to express myself. Determinism doesn't have much of a vocabulary.

In the decades since then I've learned to live with the understanding that there is no free will. All in all it has been a real positive in my life. It has taught me to accept everybody as an innocent product of nature's machinery. It has taught me to neither worship the lucky nor shun the unlucky.

But I have never forgotten the pain and the disorientation that came with my original realization. It felt like a death sentence. I luckily survived it, but I suspect that many others did not and do not.

If I had known even one happy determinist back then, my early life would have been so much easier. I would have had a model to follow. Unfortunately, I never knew a determinist of any kind, much less a happy one.

My purpose in writing this book is to provide my young self with such a model - with lots of models - with a whole community of models! Yes, my young self, this is how I want you to be. May you follow in their footsteps and be a happy, productive person.

-Secretary Michael

1. Valedictorian

✿

The high school theater is packed. Seated on stage in a single straight row and looking a bit uncomfortable in their regalia is the faculty. Facing them in the first dozen rows of the house and looking not a bit uncomfortable are the graduating seniors, so smartly dressed in their maroon caps and gowns.

The ceremony is just about over. The students have already received their diplomas and have already moved their tassels from the right side of their mortarboard caps to the left side. The school's Principal is at the lectern. She has a few last thoughts to share before inviting the valedictorian to "say farewell" (*vale dicere*) to his fellow classmates.

"My dear graduates" beams the well-liked Principal, "for nearly a century we've been holding graduation ceremonies in this beautiful theater. And each time we always have the same hopes that we feel for you today. As you know, our graduates often go out and do great things in life. They walk out of these doors and become scholars, leaders of industry, senators, inventors, distinguished achievers of all sorts. Now it's your turn. You have the power to change the world. Let me say that again. You have the power to change the world. We your teachers have given you all that we have. So take it and go change the world."

The students and guests all stand and applause. When the commotion dies down, the Principal introduces the valedictorian.

"And now for the final farewell, I'm happy to call upon our valedictorian and captain of our champion debate team, Marcus Multi."

There are cheers and then the graduates spontaneously begin chanting "Multi! Multi! Multi!" The Principal smiles and returns to her seat between the Dean of Students and the Latin teacher as Marcus Multi climbs the steps up to the stage.

When he reaches the lectern, Marcus motions with his hands to quiet his friends. He arranges his papers, pushes up his eyeglasses, and then cocks his head in a strange position as if trying to make a decision. He stands there frozen with a constipated look on his face for a good eight seconds before finally saying: "I really prepared for this." He holds up his papers and waves them a bit. "It's a good speech - at least that's what people tell me - my parents, the Principal, my teachers. And it's got some funny jokes in it." Everybody chuckles when he says this. "Some *really* funny jokes" he stresses. Everybody laughs heartily. Marcus leaves his papers on the lectern and steps down from the platform and walks to the edge of the stage. No longer at the microphone, he raises his voice so all can hear.

"I know I shouldn't go off script, but I feel that I should tell you what's really on my mind." There's a rumble of anticipation from the crowd. The Dean of Students gets ready to stand but the Principal gently tugs on his sleeve to hold him back.

"Our Principal just told us that we have power" Marcus begins. "She meant it as a compliment of course. But lately I've been thinking a lot about power. And I just don't feel that 'power' is something we should aspire to." (The teachers fidget a bit in their chairs. Some smile, some resignedly roll their eyes.)

Marcus continues: "We all know the old saying 'Power Corrupts'. It's just two words long: Power Corrupts. There's no qualifier to it. There's no 'Power *might* Corrupt' or 'Power Corrupts the *weak*' or 'Power Corrupts under this or that condition'. No. It's simply 'Power Corrupts'. Period. It's like some kind of machine. Power goes in and Corruption comes out. It's automatic. It's going to happen, good intentions or not."

"So if you believe that Power Corrupts – as I do – and if you want to avoid being corrupted - as I do - then it makes perfect *modus tollens* sense that we should avoid power. How do we do that? Simple. We should not hold-on to things that others can't have. We should not hold-on to status."

"Look at this valedictorian medal and these honor cords I'm wearing. Status. And so I take them off. Look at this golden stole embroidered with our school's coat of arms. Status. And so I take it off. Look at this cap and gown from our beloved but way too exclusive school. Status. And so I take them off." (One by one Marcus takes off items of clothing and drops them to the floor.)

"Look at this silk tie I have on with its diamond clip. Status. And so I take them off. Look at this tuxedo jacket. Status. And so I take it off. Look at these stiff shiny shoes. Status. And so I take them off. Look at this white shirt that my dear mother so perfectly ironed for me. Status. And so I take it off." (The hubbub in the audience grows, but Marcus continues.)

"Look at these tuxedo trousers. Status. And so I take them off." At this the Principal withdraws her hand from the Dean's sleeve, but it's way too late for him to stop the avalanche now. He just sits there grim-faced. Marcus is now wearing only a T-shirt, boxer shorts, and socks.

He squats down and pulls a paper out of his jacket pocket. "My acceptance into an Ivy League school?" He rips the paper in half. "Status. I'll be honored to attend our humble UMSL (*pronounced 'umsul'*) next semester." Scattered cheers erupt from his classmates.

"My 'Marcus Multi' name? Well, I love my parents dearly and I attribute all of my success to them. But our family name carries status, and so I must relinquish that too." Marcus then reaches down to a flower pot next to the lectern and scoops up a handful of dirt. He draws a large "0" on his white T-shirt with the dirt.

"From now on my name will be 'Zero'. I promise to work hard to be worthy of that name. I promise that I will do my best to be a credit to my family, to my teachers, and to all of you whom I love so much. As your valedictorian, I'm supposed to wish you all a farewell before we leave. But I'm not going to do that. There are no farewells. We're all in this together – and we must stay in this together until the end."

2. Roommates

✿

The famous Missouri Botanical Garden is made up of many smaller gardens. For example, there's an Iris Garden, a Japanese Garden, and a Daylily Garden. Una is on her way to the Herb Garden when she notices a young woman about her own age sitting on a bench in the Rose Garden. The young woman looks distraught. Her eyes and cheeks are wet.

"Can I help you?" asks Una with a concerned voice, half-sitting down next to her.

The young woman looks up, smiles a bit and in a pleasant voice answers "I'm fine, thank you."

Una lingers for a while, not quite sure what "I'm fine, thank you" really means in this situation. The young woman wipes her cheeks, puts on a brave face and adds "I like your hat."

Una chuckles and sits down next to her. "Well, you just said the magic words!" Una takes off her hat and hands it to the young woman. "I made it myself!"

The young woman examines the bowl-like hat, turning it this way and that way. "It reminds me of those Native American caps" she says.

Una chuckles again and replies "It is! And I am!" She holds out her hand to introduce herself. "My name's Una. I work here."

The young woman takes her hand and smiles. "My name's Daifu (*pronounced Die-Foo*). I'm happy to meet you, Una."

"Daifu - Daifu" repeats Una a few times, trying to get comfortable with the unusual name.

Daifu continues to admire the cap, then hands it back to Una. "It's really lovely. Thanks for showing it to me."

"You're welcome!" Una puts her cap back on. "If you have a moment, I'd like to take you to the Basketry Garden. It grows all the grasses and willows I use to make caps like this."

Daifu smiles. "That sounds interesting" she replies. As they walk towards the Basketry Garden, Daifu begins to notice the beauty of the place.

"You're lucky to have a job here, Una. It's so peaceful."

"I don't know about the 'peaceful' part, but yeah I do feel lucky working here. It was just an impulse. Last year I was studying botany at Humboldt State University. My textbook frequently referenced research done here at the Missouri Botanical Garden. So one day on a whim I just decided to move here."

"To cut out the middle man?" jokes Una

"Yes, to cut out the middle man" chuckles Daifu. And I'm glad I did. St. Louis really is the place to be for Plant Science."

"Where's Humboldt State University?"

"California - Northern California - in Arcata - near the Pacific Coast."

"Wow, it sounds beautiful!"

"It is - it really is. But I spent my whole life in that area - on the Hoopa Indian Reservation to be exact. I decided that I needed to get out and experience new things."

"So you escaped to St. Louis?" asks Daifu.

Una chuckles. "No, not 'escape'. I was happy in Hoopa - very happy. But my parents always encouraged us to stay active and explore new things. So I moved here just for the adventure of it - just to force myself to learn new things and to meet new people - people like you."

Daifu smiles. "Traveling really is an education, isn't it? A person really does grow when she moves to new places and meets new people. I still feel it."

"Then you're not from St. Louis either?" asks Una.

"No, my parents and I live in Iowa. Originally we're from Taiwan - we immigrated to the U.S. when I was twelve. The reason I'm here in St. Louis is because I won a scholarship to Washington University."

"Wow! Congratulations Daifu!"

"I know it must sound wonderful. But at the moment, I'm totally depressed about it all - especially with my roommate who came back drunk again last night. She came stumbling through the door with her moron boyfriend at three o'clock this morning. They kept me up all night with their bouncing and yelping and vomiting."

Una chuckles a little. "I love roommate horror stories."

"Oh, I could fill a whole book with this one - and I've only known her for a week! When I applied at the Housing Office, I specifically asked for a non-smoker. The first time she opened her mouth I half expected the smoke alarm to go off."

Una laughs. "I used to want a roommate to split the rent with. But after hearing so many stories like yours I feel lucky that I live alone!"

Daifu stops walking and grabs Una's arm. "Would you consider letting me be your roommate? I'm very quiet, I'm very clean, and of course I would share in the rent..."

Una wasn't expecting this, but she begins to consider Daifu's proposal aloud. "Well, with somebody sharing the rent, I might be able to sign-up for a class or two at UMSL this semester."

"I think we'd get along perfectly!" adds Daifu.

"Nobody gets along perfectly" chuckles Una. "And I have to warn you that the place where I live is more like a workshop than an apartment. I've got bundles of roots and grasses and other millinery supplies all over the place. It's in that big old building on Samaria Street. It used to be a factory before they divided it up."

"Sounds adventurous!" replies Daifu.

"Oh, it's adventurous all right - especially in winter with our maybe-I-will, maybe-I-won't radiators."

"Hey - I'm from Iowa! I can handle St. Louis winters." Then with growing desperation in her voice, Daifu pleads: "And of course I'll help with the rent, Una! I'll pay you whatever you want!"

"Daifu, if I ever go out to buy a car, remind me not to bring you along" quips Una. "But if you're really that interested, you can drop by this afternoon after I get off work and check it out."

Two days later Daifu moved in with Una. Daifu took Una's old bedroom - a bright, clean, cheerful room. Una bought a cot and set it up in her workroom amongst the buckets and shelves of woodwardia fern and other plant weaving supplies.

There are no roommate horror stories to tell about Daifu and Una. Just as Daifu had foreseen, they became the best of friends.

3. Waitress

✲

North of downtown St. Louis, the Little Sisters of the Poor operate a large residence building called the "Home" where they care for the elderly poor. Their mission is to help the elderly find purpose to their lives and freedom from worry.

Clare lives a few blocks away from the Home. She often volunteers there, spending time with the elderly and helping the Sisters with their chores. Since Clare knows how to drive their truck, she and Sister Agnes regularly make the rounds to area restaurants and bakeries, collecting leftover food. One of the main restaurants they rely on is the popular Royal Brice Steakhouse.

Late one summer afternoon, Clare stands on the Royal Brice's loading dock and knocks on the big heavy door. She doesn't have the truck with her. She doesn't have Sister Agnes with her. She doesn't even have any empty boxes with her. She's there for a very different reason.

Bert and Bernie Bernardone, the owners, look through the window then slide the delivery door open. They are surprised to see her. "Sister Clare! We weren't expecting you! C'mon in!"

Clare steps inside, hugs them as usual, and then explains her unscheduled visit. "Yesterday when Sister Agnes and I were here for the pickup, I overheard one of the staff say that you were looking to hire another server. If you're still looking, I'd like to apply."

"Oh, we'd love to have you!" they both say, noticeably pleased with the prospect of having Clare on their staff. "Our son Brice is home from college. We've put him in charge of staffing. Why don't you take a chair, Sister, and we'll send him back to meet you."

Clare has been in this storage room many, many times. But in the past she's always been in a hurry. Now as she waits for the Bernardones' son, she has time to look around. She looks at the shelves of rice, flour and other grains. She looks at the cleaning supplies so neatly stacked. It's obvious that the Royal Brice is well managed - but not perfectly so, she notes.

The door from the noisy cooking area swings open and an attractive, rather chubby fellow wearing a white apron enters holding a sheet of paper.

"Sister Clare?" he asks.

"Brice?" she asks.

"Just call me B.B." he requests. "Same nickname as my father. When there's confusion, he's B.B.Bernie and I'm B.B.Brice."

"I'm happy to meet you, B.B." she says, shaking his hand. "And you can just call me Clare. I'm not a nun."

"You don't live at the Home?"

"No, I'm just a volunteer there. I live on San Damiano."

"Oh, a volunteer! That speaks well of you. And I know my parents sure speak highly of you! Do you have any restaurant experience?"

"At the Home I often serve the residents and help keep the kitchen in order. I have a ServSafe certification."

"You have a ServSafe certification?" asks B.B. with surprise in his voice. "I hope we're in compliance" he chuckles as his eyes dart around the storage room.

"Three violations" replies Clare with a smile as she points them out. "The mop over there isn't hanging up, that rice sack isn't 6-inches off the floor, and there's a bottle of window cleaner on the shelf above the hamburger buns."

"Oh my goodness" says B.B. with an apologetic voice. He sets down his paper and immediately corrects each problem. "Do we pass now?" he asks Clare.

"With flying colors" she answers with a smile.

"Well Sister... I mean Clare..."

Clare laughs "It's okay. You can call me Sister if you want. I actually like it. I'd probably join them if I thought they'd accept me."

"Why wouldn't they accept you?"

"Well..." She hesitates for a moment, then continues. "For starters, I'm not even a theist."

B.B. laughs out loud. "Yes, I can see where that would be a problem in a Catholic convent." Then he shouts: "Barricade the doors! Here comes the atheist!"

Clare rolls her eyes a little, sorry that she has broached the subject.

B.B. picks up his paper again. "How about education?"

"I'll be a junior at UMSL. I'm majoring in Chemistry."

"Oh, I wish I could have done that. I love science. But I had to major in business because of the restaurant. By the way, Clare, why do you have a ServSafe certification?"

"Oh, I used to dream about opening my own restaurant."

"What?! A competitor to the Royal Brice Steakhouse?!" he asks with feigned outrage.

"No, I'm a vegetarian, so we wouldn't have competed with you at all."

"Barricade the doors! Here comes the vegetarian!" B.B. shouts as he bursts out laughing.

Clare rolls her eyes a little and smiles.

4. Coach

✿

The veteran teacher walks downstairs into the basement. His son is lining-up a shot on the pool table but stops and looks over when he hears his father.

"Hi, Dad! How was your first day?"

"Like all the other first days" he chuckles. But the students were sure excited to be back. It's kind of fun to be in the middle of all that energy.

"You didn't give them homework assignments on the very first day, did you?"

"Absolutely I gave them homework assignments on the very first day! They've got to get used to it - they're in high school now! How about you? Did you sign-up for classes today?

"UMSL's registration doesn't start until Wednesday. Three ball side pocket." His son hits the ball firmly but it jumps off the table onto the floor. His father grabs it and tosses it back to his son with a chuckle.

"Thanks, Dad. I was *trying* to do that. I'm getting pretty good at it."

His father laughs.

"By the way, I found some interesting classes that I'm really looking forward to this semester."

"Like what?" asks his father.

"Well, there's a Kinesiology class..."

"Kinesiology? What's that? I don't think I've ever even *heard* of the word before!"

"It's the study of how the body moves. It's something new. They didn't even offer it back in Minnesota. I'm thinking now that I'd like to be a coach. Five ball side pocket."

"A coach? What happened to Science? I've saved decades of lesson plans for you."

"I'm planning to do both, Dad. I'd like to be a coach and a Science teacher at the same time. Seven ball side pocket."

"Well, if you can get credentialed in both subject areas,

it's not a bad idea. Some schools might prefer teachers who can double-up like that. Now you've got me really curious. What other classes are you planning to take?"

"Well, besides Kinesiology, there's Modern Dance, Biomechanics, and EP. Six ball corner pocket."

"What's EP?"

"Evolutionary Psychology. I'm really into that lately." Coach stops and looks at his father. "You know, Dad, I'm starting to doubt that we even *have* a free will. In a physical world where everything's connected, a free will just doesn't make any sense. One air molecule hits another air molecule which hits the eardrum which excites a neuron which excites another neuron... It's like billiard balls. One ball hits another ball which hits another ball... Nowhere along the chain does a 'hit ball' refuse to move. Nowhere along the chain does an 'unhit ball' decide to move of its own free will."

"I've never doubted that I have a free will" interjects his father.

"What if Nicolaus Copernicus had never doubted that the sun revolves around the earth?" asks Coach with some disappointment in his voice.

"You've got me there" admits his father. "But you've got to be careful with this kind of thinking, son. It's not healthy. It can get you into real trouble."

"Why isn't it healthy to think about simple mechanics?" asks Coach as he chalks the end of his stick.

"It may be simple mechanics, but it seems that the brain has evolved some kind of blind spot to protect itself against this kind of thinking" replies his father.

"Well" declares Coach with a chuckle in his voice "there's some light coming through my blind spot - and I feel it my duty to examine it. Eight ball corner pocket."

5. Secretary

⚙

"Hello. My name's Michael and I'm a determinist."

"Hello, Michael!" the group replies - each with a friendly smile and a willingness to help me get through this.

Unfortunately this is just a fantasy. There *is* no "Determinists Anonymous" group. There *are* no friendly smiles. I'm pretty-much alone.

For those of you who are lucky enough to not know what a determinist is, let me define it: A determinist is a person who understands that there is no free will.

Coping with this new way of seeing the world has not been easy for me. But I have no doubts. The fact that there is no free will is perfectly clear to me - paralyzingly clear. The logic is as plain as day. I try to ignore it. I try to smile and walk cheerfully along a safe and familiar 'free will' road like everybody else. But my thoughts just won't let me do it. I feel like a different person.

For one thing, I can no longer judge behavior. Yesterday on my way home I saw a homeless man relieving himself in a bush next to the Royal Brice Steakhouse. I felt sorry for him. I know that sometimes the dice just happen to roll that way. At the same time, I could see a table of elegant diners sipping wine inside the steakhouse. Again, I didn't feel sorry for them. I know that sometimes the dice just happen to roll that way.

Another deterministic obsession that makes me feel different is that I see people as procreation machines. No different from ants or watermelon blossoms, I see every behavior as some kind of move to get his or her genes into the next generation. Sometimes it's easy to figure out (such as why somebody has dressed a certain way), but usually it's totally mystifying (such as why somebody would declare a major in music - which I have done).

It's hard to put into words what "disorientation" feels like. "Nausea" is a word that pretty-much sums it up. That and a racing in my mind as it spins faster and faster like one of those Fourth-of-July chasers before it explodes. I know I'm close to the edge of sanity because I can actually see the edge. I can see the abyss inching towards me, closer and closer and closer. I can't move my feet. All I can do is try to lean away from it.

But this afternoon a savior has unexpectedly arrived. I was sitting in the Music Department office (where I have a part-time student job as secretary) and was paging through the new UMSL course catalog when I noticed that an Evolutionary Psychology class was listed. This is exactly what I need in my life! EP101 - the Introduction to Evolutionary Psychology. Ever since finding it I haven't been able to stop thinking about it. Every five minutes or so I go back and read the course description again. It's like the most beautiful poem I've ever read - a poem of hope - a poem of not being alone anymore.

```
EP101:  INTRO EVOLUTIONARY PSYCH    (3 CR)
Exploration of gene-scripted behavior in
humans and animals;  Sexual selection in
everyday life; Comparative strategies for
genetic success in humans;
(T/TH 3:30 OUTBUILDING)
```

I don't know where this class came from - it just fell out of the sky like manna! It seems perfect for me despite a few weirdities about it. It's weird that the EP101 credit hours can't be applied to any degree program. It's also weird that the class is scheduled for late afternoon (which is going to really mess-up my work schedule). And why in the world did they stick the class way out in the old Caddy Shack? (UMSL used to be a golf course). It's like the administration doesn't care much about this class. But I sure do - and I'm going to take this class no matter what - even if I have to graduate a semester late - even if I *never* graduate - I'm going to take this class!

6. My Classmates

Our first EP (Evolutionary Psychology) class was on Tuesday, September 6. It was a long, hot walk from the Science Building to the grass field where the old Caddy Shack stood. The cabin-size wood building wasn't air conditioned, but it was very pleasant. All the windows were open and two large floor fans hummed from the back corners, cooling us in the fragrance of freshly cut grass.

Although I got there a bit early, there were already a number of students seated and waiting. I particularly remember a young woman who smiled at me and said "hello" as I sat down in the desk behind her. Her hair was braided into two pigtails, and she wore a hat that looked like a small, upside-down basket. "Wow, a Native American!" I thought to myself.

It was fun sitting there, watching people come in through the door. One smiling fellow came bounding in wearing a jersey with the word "COACH" displayed in large, bold letters. When he walked over to sit in the desk next to me, he patted me on the shoulder a couple of times, just like I see coaches do on TV.

A few minutes later, a cute bookwormish woman with thick glasses slipped in. I was hopeful for a moment, but she looked at no one as she stiffly rushed to the other side of the room and sat in the front desk.

A thin man wearing black-rimmed glasses and trying to grow a goatee was the next to enter. He smiled and repeatedly nodded to everybody as he found a chair in the middle row.

Soon after that, a pretty, self-confident woman wearing a waitress uniform entered. She looked at all of us, smiled, and calmly greeted us with "Good Afternoon!" as she walked over to the last row and sat behind the bookworm.

Then a man who had to be older than my grandfather entered carrying a sheaf of papers. He was dressed in a short-sleeved shirt and tie. He had one of those fascinating, weathered faces that I just couldn't stop looking at. He sat on the edge of the teacher's desk. The room grew silent. "Welcome to EP101" he said with a soft voice and a friendly smile. Our adventure had begun.

7. The First Class

✿

From that very first class, our Professor had us hooked. It started-off like most first-day classes. He took attendance and then gave us a taste of what would be on our table later in the semester. To me it was like a chef describing - in scrumptious detail - what was going to be served at the feast. My mind was salivating.

As expected, our appetizers would include brief reviews of Darwinian evolution, sexual selection, gene theory and other such staff-of-life dishes. Although I had already tasted these in other classes and in my own reading, I could never get enough of them. But what excited me the most were the main dishes - the specialty-of-the-house dishes. Among these was a dish called "Searching for Pre-Packaged Goodies" and another dish called "Lives in Reverse".

In "Searching for Pre-Packaged Goodies" we'd be looking for behaviors encoded in our genes - behaviors that we're born with - behaviors that we're ready to use straight from the box, so to speak. In "Lives in Reverse" we would rewind the lives of admired heroes and despised criminals to discover possible reasons for why they ended-up the way they did. These were the very dishes that my deterministic appetite hungered for.

Near the end of class, with only a few minutes left, our Professor asked us what *personal* goals we had for taking his class. Why had we enrolled in EP101? A few students had very practical goals. They felt the class would look good on their resumes or would help them get into graduate school. But most were like me - just plain interested in the material. We had no particular goal beyond a desire to understand it.

Then Zero, the fellow who was trying to grow the goatee, bounced the question back to our Professor. He asked our Professor if he had a personal goal for *teaching* the class.

"*My* personal goal?" chuckled our Professor. "Well I certainly *do* have a personal goal in teaching this class, but I'm so sure of reaching it that I never much think about it anymore."

He went on to compare his situation to that of a swimming

coach. He explained that if a swimming coach's goal was for his or her team to win the gold medal, then there would probably be lots of pressure, lots of worry, and in the end probably lots of disappointment. But if the swimming coach's goal was simply that each swimmer get good healthy exercise, then chances are quite high that the coach would reach his or her goal. Swimming is - almost by definition - a good healthy exercise. Getting good healthy exercise is a natural by-product of doing the activity.

"Same with me" he explained. "My goal is that you all grow to understand - to deeply understand - that everybody is equal."

He puffed his cheeks, raised his arms and shrugged his shoulders as if apologizing for the simplicity of it.

"That's it! That's my goal! And I know it'll happen - it always does. Studying Evolutionary Psychology requires - almost by definition - an understanding that everybody is equal. The study and the understanding are natural by-products of each other. It's hard to have one without the other."

The clock above the door showed that we should have ended the class five minutes ago. But nobody moved.

"So I'm not worried about reaching my goal, Zero. Thanks for asking, but it's a done deal. I'll see you all on Thursday."

I sat there a long while, quietly admiring my Professor and my classmates as they packed-up their things and headed out the door. All I could think of was "I *love* this class!"

8. The Last Class

✿

Winter came early this year. Our beautiful St. Louis autumn only lasted a few days before a deep freeze choked all the color from the leaves. Even though it is early November, I have to knock snow off of my galoshes before entering the classroom. But it sure feels nice and warm inside.

Maybe it's from the excitement of the season's first snow, but for some reason everybody seems extra chipper today. This includes Una (my Native American classmate and imaginary girlfriend with her basket hat), Coach (dressed in layers of flannel), Zero (with his now much darker goatee), Clare (in her waitress uniform beneath a long black overcoat), and even our Professor. We all seem to be charged with extra good cheer.

Our Professor explains that he has good reason to feel cheerful. He has read our midterm essays and finds them to be 'exceptional' (to use his exact word). He even calls us his 'dream class'. I sure hope he's in the same frame of mind when he's recording our final grades!

Now that more than half the semester is over, it's time for us to change gears again. We've spent the previous month looking for 'pre-packaged goodies' - behaviors that we're born with. And although looking for these 'pre-packaged goodies' was interesting enough for us to happily continue doing it forever, our course is supposed to follow a certain schedule. And that schedule now requires that we focus our attention on 'Special Topics' in Evolutionary Psychology.

Our Professor tells us that he personally has a long list of Special Topics that he'd love to explore if this were *his* class. But he makes it clear that this *isn't* his class - it's *our* class. And so he directly asks us: "Given the entire scope of Evolutionary Psychology, what Special Topics would you like to focus on during the final few weeks?"

Surprisingly, it's our reclusive bookworm Purity Jones who is the first to raise her hand. I've always been drawn to unpretentious, studious women like Purity. But there's something severe about her. Earlier when I mentioned that everybody seemed extra cheerful today, I wasn't really thinking of Purity. I've never once seen her smile. I've never once heard her chit-chat with anybody. I just can't figure her out.

"Yes, Purity?" acknowledges our Professor. "What would your Special Topic be?"

Purity replies: "I think we should discuss whether or not we have a free will. The very idea of not having one makes me feel sick and empty."

Wow! I feel like shouting "I love you, Purity!" She said exactly what I would have said - had I the courage. We must be twins or something!

"It haunts me" she adds.

Our Professor chuckles and warmly replies "As well it should, Purity! As well it should! The subject of 'determinism' has haunted many thinkers over the millennia. Good suggestion. We'll definitely spend some time discussing 'determinism'. Any other suggestions?"

Clare, the waitress sitting behind Purity, raises her hand.

"Yes, Clare?"

"I volunteer in a community where material things are *shared*, but I live in a community where material things are *hoarded*. I'd like to explore how 'hoarding' versus 'sharing' have evolved as different survival strategies."

"Another good suggestion" replies our Professor as he pulls a little notebook out of his shirt pocket and starts writing. "Hoarding versus sharing. This might give us an excuse to revisit Hamilton's Rule. Anybody else? Yes, Coach?"

"I'd like to discuss the need people have to form groups" he begins. "I'd like to explore the relative importance of these groups. For example, what's more important - the *family* group or the *religious* group - the *religious* group or the *political* group - the *political* group or the *peer* group? I'd also like to look at the *behaviors* that kick-in once somebody identifies with a group."

"Social grouping. Excellent, Coach! Any others?" Zero raises his hand. "Yes, Zero?"

"Violence - and *fear* of violence" he replies. I'd like to discuss these as survival strategies - and their genetic components, if any."

"Violence and fear of violence" repeats our Professor as he writes in his little notebook. "Wonderful. Thank you, Zero. Any other suggestions? Our Professor waits a few seconds as he looks around the room. None? Well, these should keep us quite busy. Over the weekend I'll try to prepare a schedule for the remainder of the semester. Anything else before we go? Nothing? I want to thank you once again for the thought and effort you put into your essays. Enjoy this snowy day - what's left of it. I look forward to seeing you all next Tuesday."

With that, everybody starts to put on their winter coats and gather-up their books. Since Una is already surrounded by a bevy of friends, I summon up all my courage and try to say something to Purity as she bee-lines towards the door.

"Have a nice weekend, Purity!"

She keeps walking - doesn't turn her head - doesn't say a word. Oh well.

9. No Music, Please

✿

It was the strangest request. I was sitting at the piano with my music sheets all in order. The choir was all lined-up on the risers, ready to sing. Then the pastor walks over to us and has a few words with the music director. The music director, with a confused look on her face, huddles us together and tells us that the pastor doesn't want any music during this service.

No music? I wonder if I'm still going to get paid. You see, on weekends I play the piano at two different churches and a synagogue to help pay for college. Why in the world doesn't the pastor want any music?

This church - the Church of the Free Will - has an older pastor who's normally got a great sense of humor. However it's evident that she's in no joking mood as she walks up to the pulpit.

"Good Morning" she greets the congregation with an unexpected weariness in her voice.

"Good Morning!" we answer rather cheerfully.

"I hate to start things off with bad news, but I must. Will everybody please be seated?

Those who are standing - ready to sing - all immediately sit down in a loud rustle of winter clothing. Those who are walking up and down the aisle - looking for a place to sit - settle into the nearest pew. We all give Pastor Causasui our full attention.

"This morning I got word that the young woman we were sponsoring through our student scholar program died last week - apparently by her own hand." There's an audible gasp from the congregation.

"Purity Jones was..." The Pastor's words are interrupted by several screams from the congregation. She pauses, then starts again.

"Purity Jones was our promising young scholar in whom we had invested so much of ourselves. I'm sure the lurid details of her death will soon be front page news, so there's no need to waddle in them here. Why did she do such a thing? Who knows. Maybe it had something to do with her financial troubles. Maybe it had something to do with her abduction a few years ago. Maybe it had something to do with the death of her parents or with trying to raise her young daughter alone. From the notebook she had with her, some think it maybe had something to do with the strange class she was taking at school. We'll probably never know.

But whatever the reason, no reason can ever take away the sorrow we feel here today. No reason can ever take away our deep disappointment in her. In fact from now on whenever we think of her, we probably won't remember her as the intelligent young woman that she was. No. We'll instead remember her as someone who must have been rather stupid, someone who must have been rather selfish, and above all - someone who was violent. That's because suicide changes everything.

So take note of this all you young people here today. Look at the anguish around you and remember what you are seeing. Listen to the crying and remember what you are hearing. Take-in the pain and remember what you are feeling. Suicide is not a private matter. It's a public cruelty - a public cruelty! It's a bomb that destroys everybody around. It causes pain to people who do not deserve to suffer. It empties people who do not deserve to be left empty. It steals hope and future from people who do not deserve to have their hopes and futures stolen away. So look - and listen - and feel - and burn this into your brains. Suicide is not a private matter. It is a public cruelty."

Nauseated, I slide off the piano bench and squat down on the floor with my head near the pedals so I won't faint. I can feel my old sickness returning. Like me, Purity had been accosted by determinism. Unlike me, she didn't survive it. Having once suffered that same emptiness and that same hopelessness, I understand why she didn't survive it. I understand exactly why.

10. Class Cancelled

✿

Just as Pastor Causasui had predicted, all the sensationalized details of the suicide were soon front-page news. By the time Tuesday's class rolled around, we all knew what had happened. We all knew that our Professor had been questioned by the police regarding the material he was teaching us. We all knew that he had become an object of scorn on local talk radio.

I arrive at class a couple minutes late (I'm ashamed to say). As I sneak in, I feel relieved that our Professor is not yet here. My heart sinks when I see the flowers on Purity's desk. My classmates are already deep in discussion. A couple of them greet me by name as I enter - which makes me feel good. They quickly resume their discussion.

"It's not fair that the media are linking the suicide to this class" someone says. If Purity had happened to have her grocery list with her instead of her class notes, would they be blaming Piggly Wiggly for her death? It's just not fair. Did you see that interview they had with our Professor on the news last night?"

"Interview?" objects another. "More like a public flogging!" We all concur.

"When our Professor gets here, we need to make sure - *absolutely* sure - that he feels no culpability in this" insists one fellow.

We hear footsteps on the porch and we all hush-up. An older woman wedges the door open a bit and sticks her head in.

"Excuse me, is this EP101?" she asks.

"Yes" we answer. The leaves are blowing in, so she quickly steps inside and closes the door.

"Administration has sent me over to offer you their condolences and to relay some information." She lifts her yellow notepad and begins reading: "The University Board held a special meeting this morning regarding this class. They came to two decisions: First, they decided to make free counseling available to all of you. They encourage you to take advantage of this by visiting the Student Health Center. Second, they decided to cancel this class for the rest of the semester."

Our entire class explodes in outrage. The administration woman is visibly startled.

"Please," she says. "I'm just the secretary - don't get upset with *me!*"

After expressing some apology, we ask her - in a more civil tone - why the class is being cancelled.

She continues reading from her notepad: "In place of this class, the Board has created several alternatives from which you may choose. They suggest that you meet with your academic advisor to decide which alternative would be best for you."

Then someone in back asks her directly: "Where's our Professor?"

The administration woman hesitates for a moment as if weighing which answer to give.

"My understanding is that the University lawyers have asked him to stay off campus until things get sorted out."

"You mean you fired him?!" we shout.

"I wasn't given that information" she replies.

A quiet pall fills our classroom. "Oh that dear man" whispers a woman in front.

The secretary then tells us that she has no more information and asks whether there is anything else she can do for us. We politely answer "No, thank you." She then again expresses sorrow for our loss, wedges open the door just enough to squeeze out without allowing too many leaves to blow in, and heads back towards the administration building.

After the secretary is out of earshot, Una grumbles: "Bureaucrats! There's no way this class is cancelled!" With those words our sullen class comes back to life.

"I'm with you, Una!" says Zero. "We've been through too much. We need to stick together." There's wide agreement.

Clare the waitress adds: "Plus, we've got unfinished business to take care of. We've got to figure-out what happened with Purity so we can prevent it from happening again."

There's a long pause. I feel that I know what happened to Purity. I suspect my classmates feel that they know too - at least the deterministic ones. But it's Zero who breaks the silence with a confession:

"Actually, if anybody could have helped Purity, it was me. But I just didn't realize how much pain she was in - plus she was so intimidating."

A couple chairs behind me, Corky retorts in a very matter-of-fact voice: "Zero, there was nothing you could have done. Everybody always feels guilty after a suicide. But in reality there was nothing any of us could have done."

"Actually Corky, there *was* something we could have done" replies Zero in a conciliatory tone. "That's what counseling's all about. That's what friendship's all about."

"Look Zero, the cold, hard fact is that Purity found a rope on campus last Thursday night. She walked into the Science Building, climbed up the lobby's staircase to the mezzanine, and then hung herself from the railing - hung herself right over those big brass letters that spell 'Science Makes Life Better'. There was nothing accidental about it. She knew *exactly* what she was doing. It was in the cards. And there was nothing that you or *any* of us could have done to stop her."

"But I had a real chance to do something" asserts Zero. "Last Thursday after class, I ran into Purity down by Bugg Lake and asked her if she had any plans for Thanksgiving. All she said was 'No, I don't want to sleep with you'."

Corky laughs loudly. "Classic Purity! She was the same with everybody! That's just the way she was!"

Zero continues with his confession: "But instead of recognizing that *she* had a problem, I felt that *I* had a problem - that I was just too repulsive or something."

Corky jokes: "Well, you *are* pretty repulsive, Zero." (A few laugh a little at this - which is okay because there's certainly nothing repulsive about Zero.) Corky continues: "But even if you had my good looks, you *still* would have gotten the same answer. That's just the way she was. Purity was honest - totally honest."

Several classmates object to his use of the word 'honest'. Corky retorts: "Sure! That's the whole idea behind Evolutionary Psychology, isn't it? The purpose of our behavior - of *all* our behavior - is to get our genes into the next generation. Sex is behind everything we do whether we know it or not. Purity knew it."

"She was delusional" states Zero.

"Oh come on, Zero!" taunts Corky. "You can't tell me that on some level you didn't want to have sex with her. Man, I sure did!" (This creates some commotion in the class - a mix of laughter and objection.) "Oh come on you prudes!" responds Corky. "All of you did too! Even you women!"

Zero calms the waters again with his composure. "Purity was a good student - we all know that. Maybe she just wasn't able to keep EP101 out of her everyday life. Maybe she wasn't able to turn off her deterministic thinking. Maybe she wasn't able to be a 'happy hypocrite' like the rest of us. But that inability to be a hypocrite is - I feel - a kind of mental illness. I should have seen that. It's my fault. I'm the one who aspires to be a counselor. I should have seen that. I - should - have - seen - that."

Zero then stands and faces us, speaking slowly and emphatically: "But I promise you - I promise you all - that I will never, never, never let this happen again."

We are all frozen in the moment - united in some indescribable way. One thing I know for sure: this Zero fellow will forever be one of my heroes.

The clock shows that class is over and several students start to get up to leave. Una shouts: "Stop! Nobody move!" She runs up to the chalkboard and writes her address in big letters: 185 SAMARIA STREET - LOFT 9. "This is where I live. Let's meet at my place this Sunday at twelve noon to continue this."

"And let's all bring something to eat" suggests Clare. "We can make it a pot-luck!"

"Desserts only!" shouts Coach. Suddenly we are all full of hope - even giddy! In the space of some 20 seconds, a heartbeat has returned to our beloved EP101.

11. First Meeting at Una's

That Sunday, a few days before Thanksgiving, we meet at Una's for the very first time. Out of a class of about 30, only five of us show up: Una, Zero, Coach, Clare, and me. Although we were hoping for a larger turnout - 17% is kind of disappointing - none of us are surprised that we five are the ones who ended-up together. In a subconscious sort of way, we had long ago discovered each other.

Meeting outside of school is a strange and exciting feeling. So used to seeing each other under fluorescent lighting and with a chalkboard in the background, it's like meeting for the first time. No longer are we like flat images on a flickering television screen. In the warm colors of Una's loft, everybody becomes real - deeply real - living, breathing, animal real. Una invites us to make ourselves at home. There aren't enough chairs, so we all sit in a circle on the floor.

As we wander directionless from topic to topic, we learn new and interesting things about each other:

As for Coach, we learn that he grew up on a bean farm in Minnesota - mostly kidney beans. During the economic downturn they lost the farm and had to auction it off. They were able to survive because his father reinvented himself as a science teacher and found a job here in St. Louis. We also learn that Coach organized a couple of grade school soccer teams this semester, and that last summer he danced in a production of "South Pacific" at the Muny.

As for Zero, we learn that his name used to be "Marcus" but he changed it several years ago because he wanted to start over again without any status. We already knew that he's interested in deviant behavior and that he aspires to be a psychologist, but we didn't know that he volunteers at Badluck Jail every weekend, where he mostly just talks with the inmates.

As for Clare, we learn that she's a waitress at the Royal Brice Steakhouse and that she spends lots of time volunteering with the Sisters of the Poor. The Sisters of the Poor operate a large home for the elderly poor. Their mission is to help the elderly find purpose to their lives and freedom from worry.

As for Una, we learn that she belongs to the Hupa Valley Tribe and grew up on an Indian Reservation in Hoopa California. We learn that she works at the Missouri Botanical Garden where she maintains their Basketry Garden and teaches classes in weaving and fiber dying. She also works as an independent artist, weaving her tribe's iconic bowl-shaped hats from the fragrant collection of grasses and branches that she has right here in her room!

As for me, I explain that I tune pianos during the evenings and play church gigs on the weekends. They kindly make the obligatory "oh!" sounds, but I really doubt that they're much impressed.

We talk a bit longer but I don't pay much attention because I've already learned what I had been hoping for. I learned that they all consider themselves 'determinists'. My search is finally over! I no longer feel alone!

Then Una says the magical words: "I think we should form a group so we can stay together."

"Yes!" we all excitedly answer. "Yes!" The ordeal we've gone through together during the past week has somehow given us a sense of solidarity. For some inexplicable reason, we need each other now.

"We ought to establish some goals for our group - some kind of mission" I suggest.

"Right!" replies Clare without any hesitation. "And goal Number One should be to make sure there aren't any more suicides. Let's dedicate ourselves to the memory of Purity."

"Absolutely!" agrees Zero "Let's figure out some strategy for counseling new determinists so this doesn't happen again."

"Counsel determinists? And how are we going to do *that*?" asks Una with a bit of mockery in her voice. "By telling them to stop thinking? By telling them that the laws of nature actually don't apply to them because they're so precious - so humanly precious?" We all chuckle a little. Una can be pretty sarcastic, especially with Zero.

"Zero," she continues "there's *nothing* we can tell them because there *are* no strategies for counseling determinists. Every wacko in this room is *proof* that there aren't any strategies! Them determinists are all on their own, baby - they're all on their own."

Zero, once the captain of his high school debate team, matter-of-factly responds with a slight aire of superiority in his voice: "No, they're *not* on their own, 'baby' - they're *not* on their own. They've got us."

"That's right!" bursts out Clare excitedly. "New determinists have *us* as a model! We're the evidence that everything can eventually work out! The very *existence* of our group is proof that determinism's not a death sentence."

"Not a death sentence? We can do better than that! We can make it something cool! All we have to do is be open about it and stay together as a positive force" adds Coach.

"Oh no! Now we can *never* break up" whines Una with feigned disappointment in her voice. We all laugh.

This is a happy and auspicious way to begin our first meeting together. Like the sun is able to give strength to plants just by being the sun, we feel that we can give hope to other determinists just by being ourselves - just by being visible 'out of the closet' determinists.

"So do you want to meet here again next month?" asks Una "Same time, same place?"

"Yes!" we all firmly reply.

"But not just next month" I plead, hoping not to sound too much like the needy, desperate person that I am. "Let's make this something regular! Let's meet here *every* month! What is this, the third Sunday of November? Let's meet at twelve noon on *every* third Sunday!" They all agree.

"And let's studying Evolutionary Psychology" urges Zero. "Let's keep our old class going. Maybe we can take turns giving presentations - like book reports or something."

"I'm almost finished reading *The Moral Animal*" I announce. "Maybe I could give a presentation on *that* next time."

"That would be excellent, Michael!" replies Zero. Everybody else seems pleased too. Then Una shouts "Dessert time!" With a cheer we all jump up and happily crowd around her sturdy worktable to end our first meeting with five desserts to share!

12. Fountain Room

✿

It was cold in Una's loft for our December meeting - really cold. We could see our breath as we talked. The five of us were sitting on the floor in a circle with our stocking feet together like the center of a flower.

"We need another blanket. I'll go get one from Daifu's room. Don't tell her!" says Una with a chuckle as she stands up and walks into the little bedroom.

When she returns holding the neatly folded bundle, Coach asks: "Una, did you forget to pay your heating bill last month?"

"Oh these old buildings" whines Una. "But it sure heats up nicely in the summer, so I guess I shouldn't complain." We all laugh. After she rearranges the blankets over our legs, she burrows in to join us. "Well, let's get started" she says. "Where did we leave off? Michael, I saw you taking notes last time. Would you care to be our secretary?"

"Sure!" I reply as I take some index cards out of my shirt pocket - a practice I learned from our Professor.

"At the end of our last meeting" I begin "we were setting goals for our group. So far we have two of them. Our first goal is to openly embrace determinism so that others who are struggling with it might find hope and peace through us."

"Our *raison d'être*" interjects Zero with an exaggerated French accent. Una rolls her eyes.

"Our second goal is to keep growing as Evolutionary Psychology students. Zero suggested that we take turns giving monthly presentations. I'm prepared to give mine today."

Clare's teeth are chattering as she interrupts: "Even though I enjoy playing footsie with all of you, it's too cold in here to think! Why don't we all walk over to the Royal Brice. It's warm there and I can get us all some hot chocolate. I know it'll be okay with B.B."

"To the Royal Brice!" we all happily shout. I roll-up my charts and grab the stack of hand-outs that I had prepared for my presentation. We all get up, put on our shoes (we're already wearing our coats and hats), and hike over to the Royal Brice - less than a mile away.

The Royal Brice Steakhouse is one of St. Louis's most exclusive restaurants. Clare is a waitress there and seems to be on good terms with the whole staff - especially with a fellow she always refers to as "B.B.Brice". When we get there, the main dining room is still being used to serve Sunday Brunch, but the Fountain Room is empty (as it usually is on weekends).

The Fountain Room is mainly used during the week for corporate lunches. It's a plush room with leather chairs lining both sides of a long mahogany conference table. Being walled-off from the rest of the building, the Fountain Room is surprisingly quiet. The only noticeable sound is the gentle splashing of a fountain in a corner of the room as the water tumbles into a small fish pond.

Clare leads us into the Fountain Room. Oh how nice and warm it is in here! She invites us to sit at the conference table. A few minutes later she brings each of us a tall foamy mug of hot chocolate with a dollop of whipped cream on top, serving us just like she does her corporate customers.

Coach whines: "Oh Miss? I didn't get as much whipped cream as Michael did!" Everybody laughs.

Finally we all get to meet B.B.Brice for the very first time. He's a rather chubby fellow about our age - maybe a couple years older. He walks into the Fountain Room wearing a chef's hat and carrying a large tray of cookies. "Oooo!" we all exclaim. It's like Christmas has come a week early. There are all kinds of cookies: macadamia-pineapple cookies, anise cookies sprinkled with powdered sugar, chocolate-covered pecan cookies, apricot cups, Italian amarretties, coconut macaroons - and other kinds that I can't even identify.

B.B. smiles as he places the tray on the table. "Welcome to the Royal Brice!" he says cheerfully. "My name's B.B. Sister Clare has told us all about you and we feel so honored that you've come to visit us."

Honored? How can he mean that? Here we are sitting in his comfortable chairs, getting our germs all over his hot chocolate mugs, and devouring these wonderful treats that cost who-knows-how-much. But B.B. tells us more than once that he loves Science and would have pursued it himself had he not felt obliged to study cooking and business management instead. He insists that we all come over to the Royal Brice every month after our meeting. And I'm not exaggerating when I say that he *begged* us to include him in our group. "Sure!" we reply with excitement. Our group of five has just grown to six.

After we get settled-in and comfortable in our large chairs and have our hot chocolate and cookies in front of us, we try to resume our meeting.

"Well, what should we talk about?" asks Una.

"Well, what should we talk about?" asks Clare.

"Well, what should we talk about?" asks Zero.

"Well, what should we talk about?" asks Coach.

"Well, what should we talk about?" I ask.

"This sounds like the beginning of some kind of joke" chuckles Una. "Five determinists walk into a bar and ask what they should talk about."

I'm about to suggest that we name our group 'The Determinists' when Coach says:

"Well, one thing that I *don't* want to talk about - *ever* - is determinism. Talking about determinism is just useless. There's not even a vocabulary for it!"

"Hear, hear!" shouts Zero. "I don't want to talk about determinism either. A person either sees it or a person doesn't see it. We happen to see it. That's fine. Most other people *don't* see it. That's equally fine. I don't want to argue it yes or no."

"I don't want to argue it either" agrees Clare. "And no proselytizing! If somebody doesn't understand determinism, then good for them! If anything, we should envy them!"

By now I'm feeling really uneasy and worried that my 'dream family' of determinists is starting to fall apart. I plead: "What do you mean 'no talking about determinism'? Determinism's *all* I want to talk about! How can a group of determinists not talk about determinism? It doesn't make sense! It's like a group of plumbers not talking about water!"

"But plumbers *don't* talk about water, Michael" replies Coach with a chuckle. "They're way beyond that. They already know what water is. They just have to control it."

"Don't worry, Michael" counsels Zero. "We're all science-minded. We're not abandoning determinism. We're just tired of explaining ourselves and defending ourselves. Like Coach said, we're beyond that now."

"It's like the sun" continues Coach with another analogy. "We know it's there. There's no need for us to stare at it - in fact it isn't healthy to stare at it. We just let the sun illuminate our way. The same with determinism - we just let it illuminate our way. Like a flashlight, we can turn it on when we need to see where we're going. But most of the time we can leave it turned off."

Whew! I feel so relieved that my friends haven't turned their backs on determinism - in fact they seem to be a step ahead of me. I wish this conversation could go on forever. But when our mugs are empty, Una draws our discussion to a close so that I'll have enough time to give my presentation.

When Una introduces my topic, I get up, unroll my charts, and try my best to explain what I had learned from the Robert Wright book 'The Moral Animal'. I had really spent a lot of time preparing for this presentation, so I was happy when the others started asking questions and discussing it amongst themselves - just like we used to do with our Professor.

I miss our old Professor. I often wonder where he is and what he is doing. I raise my cup to you, old friend, and thank you for all you have given us.

13. Pajama Circle

✿

Our January meeting is almost as cold as our December meeting was - but this time we're prepared: pajamas! Last month Una told us about a sale on thick thermal pajamas that she and her roommate wear to get through the winter. The pajamas have feet and a hood, so they're quite toasty. Today we're *all* wearing them! And with a few extra blankets piled on our circle, we're all quite comfortable as we begin our third meeting.

Una starts by welcoming B.B.Brice to our group, a welcome that we all enthusiastically echo. B.B. seems happy to be here, but I must say that he looks almost as ridiculous as I feel with these pajamas on. It seems that the only pajamas available on the reduced price sale table were the leftover ones - the fluorescent greens and the electric pinks that nobody else wanted.

Then Una asks the Secretary (me) where we had left off last month in our discussion. I glance at my index cards and answer: "By the end of our last meeting we had agreed to not dwell on determinism but rather to use it as a flashlight - to use it when we need to illuminate dark places that we aren't otherwise able to see."

"And there definitely *are* dark places that we aren't otherwise able to see" interjects Zero. "And these are the places that I definitely *want* to see!"

"Then let's discuss these places" suggests Una. "What can we see with the light of determinism that we can't otherwise see?"

It's interesting that we're diving into Lake Determinism when just last month everybody wanted to stay away from it. But even though the lake can be toxic, there's something that draws us there. Just as radiation can be used to treat cancers, and just as botulism toxin can be used to treat muscle contractions, we intuitively understand that these poisonous waters can be healing.

"Well for me the biggest insight that comes from determinism has to do with blameworthiness" begins Coach. "If people are destined to do what they're going to do, then nobody is blameworthy of anything."

"Yeah, that's the big one" confirms Zero "That's the elephant in the room."

"And if nobody is blameworthy of anything, then nobody is punishment-worthy of anything" reasons Clare.

"And the water gets deeper and deeper" chuckles Coach.

"What does it mean if nobody is punishment-worthy?" asks Zero.

"Well it doesn't mean that we should empty the jails" asserts Una.

"Yes it does" interrupts Zero self-assuredly. "That's exactly what it means." (Having witnessed Zero deliver a forensic *coup de grace* to Una several times now, I'm starting to suspect that he enjoys doing it.)

"But punishment - reasonable punishment - can be constructive" argues Clare. "It helps shape behavior."

"Obviously I'm not saying that people who are a danger to others should be allowed to roam the streets" returns Zero. "But the cages have got to go. Surely we can design a system where dangerous people can be kept separate while they have a chance to grow and live decent lives - just as we would want for ourselves. Separate but equal."

"Separate but equal" repeats Una. "Yeah, that sounds like a winner. It sure worked out well for public education, didn't it?" We all chuckle a little, knowing her sarcasm is meant more for Zero than for the substance of his argument.

For quite a while longer we talked about 'blameworthiness'. We decided that in the light of determinism, the word 'blame' didn't make much sense. We agreed that we should drop the word - and other words like it - from our collective vocabulary.

With our discussion over, we pull our clothing over our pajamas and head off to the Royal Brice for our hot chocolate and cookies.

Like last time, the Fountain Room feels so nice and warm when we enter. We can't help but to make "ah!" sounds.

It's Clare's turn to give the presentation. She's brought a VCR projector with her. After we're all warmed-up with hot chocolate and cookies, B.B. asks: "Sister Clare, can I plug that in for you?

"Thanks" she answers as she throws him the end of the power cord.

For some reason, B.B. always calls her 'Sister Clare'. Since she doesn't seem to mind, the rest of us sometimes call her 'Sister Clare' too.

For her presentation today, Sister Clare has brought us a film about Charles Darwin. I think I can speak for everyone in our group when I say that Charles Darwin is one of our heroes. His writings about evolution infuse all that we do. But even if Charles had lost his manuscript on the way to the printers and had ended-up contributing nothing to our understanding of evolution, we'd still admire him for his lifelong, dogged work of trying to figure things out through careful observation.

We all enjoy watching the film. In fact it's so inspiring that no one's totally surprised when Coach suggests: "Why don't we call ourselves the 'Darwinians'!"

Having just watched a film about Darwin, I'm not sure we're all thinking clearly. Films have a way of altering consciousness. I've often caught myself driving home too fast after watching a movie at the theater. Films should have a warning label: "Don't operate dangerous machinery or make important decisions after watching this." Anyway, Coach's proposal sounds pretty good to us, so we all agree to call ourselves the 'Darwinians'.

"Of course it's not the most original name" adds Coach as he seems to reconsider. "People all over the world call themselves 'Darwinians'."

"But people all over the world call themselves 'Darwinians' because of Charles" replies Una. "We're calling ourselves 'Darwinians' because of Emma! We're 'Emma Darwinians'!"

We all erupt in cheerful agreement when Una says this. There's something exciting and even liberating in this recognition. Not to take anything away from Charles, but his wife and cousin Emma was clearly his enabler. According to the film, Charles always had lots of health problems - even when he was young. But Emma took care of him. Even though she was a religious person with a very different way of seeing the world, she took care of him. Without her nurturing, without her tolerance, without her character, we might have never even *heard* about this fellow named

Charles Darwin.

14. Corky Comes

✿

February. The temperature inside Una's room feels just as cold today as it did last month. But after crawling into the pajama circle with all my friends, I once again feel warm and connected. This month I brought a notebook with me. Writing on those little index cards just wasn't working anymore. Earlier this morning I transcribed all my cards into this spiral-bound notebook and carefully inked the name "Darwinians" on the front cover with the precision of a draftsman.

Una always sets her alarm clock to ring at noon. She's pretty good about starting on time. When it rings, she reaches over to the window sill and silences it. It's one of those old white electric clocks with a little light bulb in it - the kind my grandparents have. Una smiles at us and announces:

"Welcome to the 4th meeting of the Darwinians. Secretary Michael, where did we leave off?"

I take a glance at my new notebook and reply: "The last thing we discussed in our January meeting was whether or not the concept of 'blame' makes any sense in the light of determinism. We decided that it did *not* make any sense and we agreed to stop using words like 'blame' or 'innocent' or 'guilty'.

"We can all blame Zero for that one" quips Una.

Everybody chuckles, except for Zero who continues in a serious tone: "Actually there are *lots* of words we should probably drop from our vocabularies. And since words lead to actions, maybe we should start getting rid of all the words that are incompatible with determinism."

Just then the big old factory door swings open and a blast of cold air swooshes through us. "Corky!" we exclaim as our old EP101 classmate walks in and closes the door behind him. At first I don't recognize him with all the weight he's put on. But when I hear his gentle Corky voice and see his friendly Corky smile, it's unmistakable who he is. He comes over and looks at our pajama circle.

"What's this, an orgy?" he asks.

"Welcome to the Darwinians!" we say, inviting him to take his shoes off and get under the blankets to get warm.

"Wow, you've really gone psychedelic on me! Zero in pink, Michael in purple, and who's this fellow in pumpkin orange?"

"My name's B.B. - I'm happy to meet you!"

Corky reaches over and shakes B.B.'s hand, then turns to the women. "And my yellow foxes! Well, you two would look sexy in *any* color - or in no color at all if you catch my drift!"

"Come in and get warm!" we urge him.

"I hope I'm not interrupting anything" he says as he takes his shoes off.

"No, we were just starting to look for words that are incompatible with determinism - words that we should probably drop from our vocabularies" explains Zero.

"What if our lexicons shrink down to nothing?" jokes Sister Clare.

"*My* lexicon sure hasn't shrunk!" bursts out Corky with a hearty laugh as he points to the sexual bulge in his pants. I reflexively avert my eyes to protect his privacy as Corky squeezes himself between the women. Behind his back, Una and Clare smile and exchange "This guy's a lunatic" glances with each other as he scoots in.

From this point forward, I can't say that I took very good notes. Zero of course keeps on talking about vocabulary words - continuing as if nothing unusual has happened. But I sense that something unusual has indeed happened. I sense that something is wrong with Corky.

After our meeting we all walk over to the Royal Brice as always. It's Una's turn to give the presentation. She gives a report on Richard Dawkin's book "The Selfish Gene". Everybody seems completely enthralled and locked onto her every word. First Una explains what life looks like from a gene's point of view, and then she introduces us to something called a 'meme'. Although everybody else finds it electrifying, I just can't focus. Across from me Corky rubs his thighs and ogles the women's bodies.

15. Hat Contest

✿

March is the cruelest month. One day she smiles and gives us a sunny warmth that fills everybody with hope, then she mockingly laughs and plunges us into a cold gray depression that lasts for days on end. That's how it is today. Even though spring will be here in a couple of days, St. Louis is cold and gray.

Coach, Una and I are already in our pajama circle. I guess a pajama circle really isn't necessary today. It's cold but not freezing cold like it usually is. With warmer weather coming, this will probably be our last time. Too bad. It's the only part of winter that I'm going to miss.

I look over at the clock on the window sill and see that it's almost noon. Wow, where is everybody? As if on cue, the old factory door swings open and Zero walks in. As we greet him, Una's alarm starts ringing. She reaches over and shuts it off, and then Sister Clare slips through the door.

"Made it!" she shouts with an exhausted laugh. After she catches a few restorative breaths she adds "B.B.'s got the flu - he won't be coming today."

"The flu" we repeat with sympathetic sighs. We all know that this year's flu is no fun.

"Corky won't be coming either" adds Zero.

"Why? What happened to Corky?" asks Una.

Zero hesitates, then answers: "He's been arrested."

"Arrested?!"

"Possession of child pornography."

"Man, that guy's got a major libido problem" replies Coach.

"He's always been on the horny side, even in EP101" adds Una. "But now it just seems to be out of control."

"We're determinists - *everything* is out of control" retorts Zero. "But we need to stick with him. We might be the only friends he has."

"Especially now" adds Clare.

"Yeah, especially now" repeats Zero.

"Where is he?" asks Coach.

"Badluck Jail. I just happened to notice his name on the roster yesterday. I set up a visit session with him, but even there in the visitor's room he seemed obsessed with sex. Something's wrong. I'm wondering if he might have a tumor or something. I left a note for the resident psychologist - a friend of mine. Hopefully she can get a brain scan scheduled."

As I listen to my friends discuss this, I'm really moved. At a break in the discussion, I summon-up my nerve and say: "Sometimes I feel that I don't belong in this group."

"Sometimes *we* feel that you don't belong in this group either" replies Coach. Then he quickly adds "Just joking, Michael! I couldn't resist the setup!" Everybody laughs - including me.

"No, I'm serious" I continue. "You're all so much more mature than I am. Instead of assuming he was sick, I assumed that he was being a jerk."

"That's okay - we all have feelings like that, Michael" replies Una. Just so we don't let any of them get out. That's all that counts."

"Jerk. We should add that to our list of forbidden words" suggests Zero.

Sister Clare points out: "We're using it as a Fundamental Attribution Error, so it's already forbidden."

"What's a Fundamental Attribution Error?" I ask.

"Michael, weren't you paying attention last time?" she scolds with a smile. "It's when we attribute someone's bad behavior to some *internal* weakness rather than look for the *external* cause. Like if some guy's late for work and we just assume that he's lazy rather than check to see if the bus was running behind schedule. That's a Fundamental Attribution Error."

"Which reminds me, Clare" interjects Una in the comical tone of a suspicious schoolmaster. "Why were *you* late today? Was the bus running behind schedule?"

"No, I'm just lazy" answers Clare without hesitation. Everybody laughs.

We continue to talk about the Fundamental Attribution Error and its relevance to us as determinists. Then during a lull in the conversation, Coach's stomach rumbles. He looks down at his stomach, holds his finger to his lips and whispers "Shh! Be quiet!" We all laugh.

Coach then says: "It just wants some cookies. But I guess we won't be going to the Royal Brice today. I mean, we can't very well just show up there without B.B. and demand that they feed us." We all agree with a chuckle.

"Oh, they wouldn't mind" says Clare casually as she stretches her pajama legs under the blankets. Then she adds "But it was B.B.'s turn to give the presentation today, so there's really not much reason to even go there."

"I wouldn't have been able to go anyway" says Una. "I've got to be downtown by 2:00. In fact, I better start getting ready now" she says as she scoots out from under the blankets.

"Can we go with you?" I ask Una.

"Sure, if you want to" she replies with some uncertainty in her voice. The four of us are quite certain that we want to go with her. We know that she's being awarded a prize at the Milliner's Convention for a hat she created last year. And so we all get up from our circle, get out of our pajamas, and leave together for the downtown Convention Center where the St. Louis Millinery Association is holding its annual conference.

Every March (when the Easter bonnets and spring hats go on sale) milliners from across the country come to St. Louis to share information, take classes, find buyers, and display their art. Today, the final day of the conference, a Milliner Award will be given to the ten milliners who created the ten winning hats. This is the second year in a row that Una has won a prize (although only the first year that she's been in St. Louis to receive it).

The actual judging took place several months earlier. A panel of judges selected ten favorite hats from among the many works submitted from across the country. Today is just the award ceremony. Although there's no money associated with winning a Milliner Award, the honor of winning one is a big deal to professional milliners.

To Una, weaving her hats is more than just a job. She considers it part of her heritage. When she was a girl growing-up on the Hoopa reservation in northwestern California, her grandmother taught her the craft of making the famous basket-hats that so distinguishes her Hoopa Valley tribe. Una once told me that she loves to get lost in her hat-weaving because she can feel the presence of her grandmother when she does so.

When we arrive at the Convention Center's auditorium, Una heads for the backstage area while we look for a place to sit in the audience. It's a large space - probably seating a thousand people or so - and it's quite full, especially with college art students.

Along the front of the stage are ten pedestals, spaced equally apart. On each pedestal there's a transparent mannequin head – and on each mannequin head there's a winning hat.

"That *last* one looks like one of Una's hats, doesn't it?" asks B.B. as he points to the very last pedestal.

"It's either that or a trash can" quips Coach. We all break out laughing. It's a good thing Una can't hear us. She and the other nine winners are all backstage behind the curtain.

It's time to start. A tuxedoed Master of Ceremonies – speaking with a proper British accent – welcomes us to the 59th annual presentation of the Milliner Awards. After saying some nice words about the event's inception in 1907 and the long, glorious history of the St. Louis Millinery Association, he starts the ceremony ("without further ado") by announcing the first of the ten award winners.

Kenneth Kopf, an older man, emerges from an opening in the back curtain. He walks over to the pedestal that displays his hat as we all applaud. The Master of Ceremonies asks him some questions about his life, about his work regimen, and about his purpose and method of creating his winning handwork. It is interesting to hear his story. Afterwards the emcee hands him his award, we applaud some more, and Mr. Kopf returns backstage.

The Master of Ceremonies then calls the next winner, Thomas Testa. Mr. Testa seems quite elderly too. I guess it takes years to develop expertise in the millinery arts. One by one the winners come out to shine in the spotlight, only to again disappear behind the black curtain a few minutes later.

Una is the last to be called. By this time the audience is growing tired and doesn't applaud as much anymore. But we more than make up for it! When Una appears from behind the curtain, we whoop and holler as if she were a rock star. She looks over at us and rolls her eyes. After Una answers the emcee's questions and receives her award, she disappears behind the curtain again with all the others.

The Master of Ceremonies then explains to us that there is still one more prize to give out – the '**Top Hat Award**' – the prize that we the audience get to vote on. He tells us: "It'll be *your* job to choose the winner of that final prize. You the audience will be asked to choose, by acclamation, your favorite of these 10 hats."

Everybody is startled as a young hooligan swaggers into the auditorium from the restrooms, wearing a toilet seat around his neck and a toilet plunger on top of his head. (I know I shouldn't be using the word "hooligan" - it's a Fundamental Attribution Error word if there ever was one. But this guy more or less already has the word stamped on his forehead.)

"LOOKY ME! I GOTTA HAT TOO!" he shouts as he approaches the stage. Stunned, nobody in the auditorium makes a sound.

"LOOKY ME! I GOTTA HAT TOO!" He then lifts the plunger a couple of times while making a '*Toot-Toot*' sound as if the plunger were a train whistle.

Thinking that maybe this is part of the program, the audience responds with a brief, insecure laugh.

"THINK I'M A WINNER?" he shouts as he jumps up onto the stage.

The poor Master of Ceremonies doesn't quite know what to do. "Excuse me" he politely suggests.

The young man cheerfully responds: "YOU'RE EXCUSED!"

The audience laughs a little at this.

"THINK I'M A WINNER?" he shouts out again.

Except for a bit of laughter, the audience still doesn't respond.

"Who *are* you?" pleads the Master of Ceremonies.

"WHO ARE I? WHO ARE I?" He then looks out to the audience and shouts "I'M THE TOILET MAN!"

This time there's a bit more laughter and some clapping from the younger people in the audience.

"I'M THE TOILET MAN!" he repeats.

There's even more laughter and clapping.

"AND I AM? (*short pause*) BECAUSE I AM!" He then starts to make a catchy beat-box rhythm with his mouth.

"C'MON, HELP-OUT THE TOILET MAN!" he shouts, encouraging the audience to join him making the mouth rhythm (as the younger ones increasingly do). I know we should probably all stand up and walk out of the auditorium. But the emcee has been so smarmy and officious up to now that the shabby hooligan with his mental problems somehow seems more genuine in comparison. It kind of reminds me of the musical "Hair" when the character Berger gets up and starts dancing on the banquet table.

"THAT'S IT!" he shouts as the audience grows stronger and stronger with their beat-box sounds. Then the hooligan begins rapping in rhythm to their background rhythm:

I AM THE TOILET MAN – AND I AM BECAUSE I AM.
I AM THE TOILET MAN – AND I AM BECAUSE I AM.

DO YOU UNDERSTAND?" he shouts at the top of his lungs.
"Toilet man!" we answer.
"DO YOU UNDERSTAND?" he shouts again.
"Toilet man!" we answer.

He continues in rhythm:
"I NEVER ASKED TO HAVE THIS BODY
NEVER ASKED TO HAVE THIS MIND
NEVER ASKED TO LOOK THE WAY I LOOK
THIS FRONT OR THIS BEHIND (he slaps his hip)

I NEVER ASKED TO BE A SINNER
NEVER ASKED TO BE A SAINT (then with a driven voice:)
NEVER ASKED THAT I BE WHO I IS
OR NOT BE WHO I AIN'T

I AM THE TOILET MAN – AND I AM BECAUSE I AM.
I AM THE TOILET MAN – AND I AM BECAUSE I AM.

DO YOU UNDERSTAND?" he shouts out
"Toilet man!" we shout back.
"DO YOU UNDERSTAND?" he shouts out again
"Toilet man!" we shout back.

"I KNOW YOU DREAMED FOR SOMEONE PERFECT
PERFECT HEIGHT AND PERFECT WEIGHT
PERFECT EYES AND NOSE AND SMILING LIPS
YOU DREAMED THE PERFECT MATE

I KNOW YOU DREAMED FOR ONE TO MEET YOUR NEEDS
AND FIT INTO YOUR SLOT (then with a driven voice:)
BUT HONEY THROW THEM DREAMS AWAY
'CUZ I IS WHAT YOU GOT!

I AM THE TOILET MAN – AND I AM BECAUSE I AM.
I AM THE TOILET MAN – AND I AM BECAUSE I AM.

DO YOU UNDERSTAND?"
"Toilet man!" we shout back.
"DO YOU UNDERSTAND?"
"Toilet man!" we shout back.

"I DON'T WANT YOUR EMPTY SMILE
I DON'T WANT YOUR LITTLE SNACK
I DON'T WANT YOUR DIRTY MONEY
(then with a straight, businesslike voice:)
NO WAIT – I TAKE THAT BACK

I DON'T WANT YOUR SYMPATHETICS
I DON'T WANT YOUR DROOPY EYES
(then with a driven, relentless voice:)
I ONLY WANT A CHANCE TO LIVE
– A CHANCE TO WIN THE PRIZE

I AM THE TOILET MAN – AND I AM BECAUSE I AM.
I AM THE TOILET MAN – AND I AM BECAUSE I AM.

DO YOU UNDERSTAND?"
"Toilet man!" we shout back.

"DO YOU UNDERSTAND?"
"Toilet man!" we shout back.

"I AM THE TOILET MAN – AND I AM BECAUSE I AM.
I AM THE TOILET MAN – AND I AM BECAUSE I AM."

The hooligan then walks over to the trophy stand, grabs the Top-Hat Award, and triumphantly lifts it up high as the entire audience roars and cheers in approval.

16. Lasagna

April. The daffodils along the highways and the fruit trees in people's yards are all in blossom. St. Louis is awash in fragrance and beauty.

Inside Una's apartment there's a surprise that greets us. A large yellow banner with bold black letters spelling "The Darwinians" hangs from her vaulted ceiling and displays itself all the way down to the floor. At the top of the banner is a drawing of Emma Darwin. It isn't the Emma of the familiar water color portrait by George Richmond, lovely as it is. No, Una has 'unprissified' Emma, has tied back her hair, has put her in working clothes, and has drawn her with the strength of character that she obviously had. A fresh breeze from Una's open window plays with the cloth, snapping it this way and that. It's stunning. We all thank and compliment Una for her artistry.

We're sitting in our circle, small-talking, admiring the new banner, and waiting for the alarm to ring. Pajamas are no longer part of our uniform. Spring is here - our sweaters are more than enough.

B.B. raises his voice to make an announcement: "I'm prepared to give my presentation today. Sorry I wasn't here last time. I guess you know I was sick."

"Food poisoning?" asks Coach. We all break into loud laughter.

"No, I had the flu that was going around" he replies.

Una's alarm starts ringing. She reaches over, turns it off, smiles and declares: "Welcome to the sixth meeting of the Darwinians. Any announcements before we get started?"

"Yes, I've got an update about Corky" says Zero. "He really *did* have a tumor. (There's a sympathetic sigh from all of us.) He's scheduled for surgery later this week at St. Louis University Hospital."

"Well, I think we all suspected that *something* was wrong" says Coach.

"Can we visit him?" asks Sister Clare.

"I doubt it. He'll probably be in a restricted area. But I'll keep you all posted" replies Zero.

"Yeah, we've got to support ol' Corky" says Sister Clare.

"At least now we know that when he was here last time, he wasn't really himself" I say.

"Oh, he wasn't?" asks Coach. "Then who was he?"

"You know what I mean - he wasn't in his right mind."

"Oh, he wasn't?" continues Coach. "And what would be a right mind? One like yours?"

"One that doesn't have a tumor growing in it."

"Michael, we all have tumors in our brains. The only difference between Corky and the rest of us is that his tumor is visible and it has the name 'tumor'."

"Well, you've got a point there" I say. (I concede as quickly as I can because I actually prefer Coach's side of the argument.)

"I hope the jury thinks more like Michael and less like Coach" adds Sister Clare.

"I hope Michael thinks more like Coach and less like Michael" I straightforwardly say. Everybody chuckles.

"I've got an announcement to make" says Una with a smile. "Last November at the funeral you probably heard that Purity had a 3-year-old daughter. Well, I'm thinking of adopting her."

Wow! We all make happy and congratulatory sounds with our voices, but we're all stunned - at least I am.

"Her name's Twimfina [*twim-FEE-nuh*]. Missouri Children's Services are sorting things out now. I should find out this week if they'll let me have her. Oh, by the way, I listed all of you as references - I hope you don't mind."

"No, of course not!" we reply.

"I know what you're thinking - a suicide mother and a rapist father, this kid's a walking time bomb" continues Una as her eyes begin to well up with tears and her natural smile becomes strained and forced. Then with a voice that breaks into a whisper, she says "But things are about to change for little Twimfina - things are about to change big time." Una excuses herself and walks away to regain her composure.

During this most unexpected breakdown by the most unexpected person to have it, B.B. softly suggests: "Why don't we all go over to the restaurant now. Zero, maybe you could stay here with Una until she's ready."

Zero nods his head as we all get up off the floor.

Walking to the Royal Brice Steakhouse is exciting in this windy weather. The fruit trees are dancing like cheerleaders with their white and pink pom-poms. "Hooray for St. Louis!" they shout. But this profligate display makes it all too clear that our fruit trees are rather foolish creatures. Last year all their blossoms got wiped out by a late freeze. Now this year they're all coming out to party again as early as they did last year! They never learn. But as I look up higher than the fruit trees, high up at our Missouri natives - the oaks, the hickories, the maples - I see that they don't have even a single leaf on them yet. They're the smart ones. "Haste makes waste" as my father always says.

We all stop to look at an unusual shrub with deep red blossoms, wondering what it is. While we examine its flower structure, Zero and Una catch up with us. All six of us are together again.

When we get to the Fountain Room, we all take a seat around the conference table as usual and await our favorite cookies and hot chocolates. But when B.B. enters from the kitchen, he's carrying a large metal baking pan covered with foil.

"Wow! What's this?" we wonder with raised eyebrows. We can already smell that it's something delicious. B.B. smiles as he sets it on the table and pulls back the foil. We all gasp: "Lasagna!"

"Not *just* lasagna, brothers and sisters, not *just* lasagna. It's *vegetarian* lasagna – made with spinach! Today we're going to do a dissection" he announces as Sister Clare sets a stack of plates next to him and hands each of us a silverware wrap.

"A dissection?" we repeat curiously.

With a large stainless steel pancake turner, he gently slides a large piece of lasagna onto the first plate and hands it to Una. "Here momma, you get the first one" he says. We all warmly agree.

After we all have our plates of lasagna in front of us, B.B. holds his plate up and with his fork he curls back the top corner of his lasagna.

"This first layer here is made with mozzarella" he explains.

"It comes from Italy." He then urges us to follow along, repeating with our own lasagna. "This nutmeg sprinkled on top comes from Indonesia." He then peels back another layer.

"These special noodles are made fresh right here at the Royal Brice." He then folds back some of the vegetables. "This is Japanese eggplant. And these organic Roma tomatoes are grown right here in Missouri!"

"The sauce has lots of ingredients. It's got olive oil that comes from Spain and it's got black pepper that comes from Viet Nam... The point I want to make is that the individual layers, taken out of context, might not seem all that appetizing. In fact you might be tempted to scrape some of them off your plate. But that would be a big mistake, brothers and sisters, a big mistake! Because eaten together, layer on top of layer, they all come together as a rapturous feast."

"Rapturous!" we repeat blissfully as we take our first bites.

"I've prepared this lasagna to remind us of a principle that I hope we can embrace as a group. It's compatible with determinism and maybe even flows from it." explains B.B. "Instead of layers of lasagna, think of layers of people and layers of culture. The principle is this:

'Different people, living different lives, have different truths that they hold sacred. As long as these truths are nonviolent and aren't being forced onto others, we will respect them.'

"What do you mean by 'different truths'?" asks Zero.

"Well Brother Zero, the 'different truths' could be anything. They could be "pre-packaged goodie" truths that we're born with, or they could be tribal truths, religious truths, personal truths – anything!"

"But what if the truths aren't true?" asks Zero.

"That's just it, Brother Zero. That's just what I want us to accept – that *all* sacred truths are true. They might not jibe with the measurable, physical truths that we get from science, but they're true nonetheless.

"But B.B., what if their truths conflict with ours?" I ask.

"Well, we can't *let* them conflict, Brother Michael" he answers. "We've got to allow space for multiple truths. It's like they're on different layers of the lasagna. If we make room for them, I feel that our lives will be richer and more delicious."

"As delicious as a Royal Brice lasagna?" asks Coach.

B.B. hesitates for a moment. "Well, maybe not quite *that* delicious!" he says. We all laugh. B.B.'s always been proud of his dishes.

As we eat our wonderful lasagna, there's less talking. After a long stretch of silence, B.B. says: "Maybe this wasn't the best analogy."

"Are you kidding?" roars Coach "The analogy's the best part! In fact I think I'll have another piece of analogy!" We all laugh.

Although I'll always be a scientist, I personally aspire to this "Acceptance of Multiple Truths" principle. I *want* to respect everybody's religious beliefs. I *want* to respect the superstitions and the horoscopes and the fortune-tellings that people cling to. And I want to respect all these divergent, contradictory layers all at the same time. I want to get sustenance from the most flavorful lasagna that ever came out of the oven. I know I can do this! I may not quite be there yet, but the very challenge of it enriches my life.

17. Twimfina and the Ethics of Luck

✿

On this May morning I knock on Una's door about ten minutes before noon as I always do on the 3rd Sunday of the month. But this time a little girl opens the door, holds out her hand, and matter-of-factly says: "Hello, my name's Twimfina."

Not having had much experience with young children, I'm rather at a loss for what to do. I take her hand, bow a little, and say "I'm happy to meet you, Twimfina. My name's Michael." Then I go to my usual place in the circle, just counterclockwise from Una, feeling embarrassed for having introduced myself to a preschooler as if she were a senior diplomat.

Fortunately the others have a better sense of what to do. When Zero, Sister Clare and B.B. arrive, they all joyfully kneel down and hug Twimfina as if she were their favorite niece. When Coach arrives a few minutes later and is greeted by the same "Hello, my name's Twimfina", he reaches down, picks her up and playfully swings her high into the air, saying something like "You mean Twimfina the flying girl?" Twimfina laughs - as do the rest of us.

When the alarm announces that it's time for our meeting to begin, Una turns to Twimfina and asks her to go into Daifu's bedroom to draw some pictures for a while, which she cheerfully does. Then Una turns to us and announces: "Welcome to the 7th meeting of the Darwinians."

"Having just been bowled over by Twimfina, we're definitely not ready to talk about determinism yet. "Oh what a precious child you have!" is the gist of what we all say to Una. Una always maintains a pleasant but contained demeanor. But today I sense that her container is about to burst with joy. We all want to know more:

"How old is she now?" asks Sister Clare.

"She just turned four on May 2nd - a week before we got her."

"You adopted her during exam week?" asks Coach.

"Yeah it wasn't the best timing, but it all worked out okay" answers Una. "Daifu did a lot of babysitting for me. I always knew this might happen during exam week, so I prepared for my finals early in the semester. I think I did well on them."

"How about work?" asks B.B.

"Oh, I always take her to work with me - nobody minds - I'm not on a clock. Besides, Twimfina helps me pull the weeds and do the watering, so they're getting two for the price of one."

"Have your parents seen her yet?" asks Sister Clare.

"Next month they will. That reminds me, I won't be here for our June meeting - we'll both be in Hoopa. You're free to meet here of course, but I was wondering if you might prefer to meet in the library instead."

"The library?" we reply. Evidently none of us had ever before considered this possibility.

"If we were to meet at the library, we could still walk to the restaurant afterwards" points out B.B. "In fact we'd even be closer to it."

"The public library - hmm. Maybe if we were to advertise or somehow spread the word, we might be able to pick up some new members there" says Zero as he considers the opportunity.

"If you want, I could drop by the library tomorrow and reserve the meeting room" I say. Everybody seems pleased with the offer.

"Good" says Una. "Now that that's resolved, let's get to work. Secretary Michael, where did we leave off?"

This time I don't need to look at my notebook. "Lasagna!" I exclaim as I glance over at our smiling B.B. "Multiple layers of lasagna to represent multiple layers of truth - all of which we accept."

"And all of it delicious!" adds Coach. Everybody agrees.

"But before that" continues Una "I think we were trying to think of special insights that determinism allows us to see. Can anybody think of any other insights?"

We're all silent for a while, until I suggest: "Heroes and villains. It doesn't make sense to have heroes and villains. Determinism shows us that everybody's place in life is just a matter of luck."

There seems to be general agreement. Coach later interjects:

"In this world of no free-willin'
There ain't no hero and there ain't no villain"

We politely chuckle. Coach can come up with some weird stuff.

"I agree that everybody's place in life is a matter of luck" says B.B. It reminds me of that rhyme:

> *Rich Man, Poor Man, Beggar Man, Thief,*
> *Doctor, Lawyer, Indian Chief*

We could have been any of them!"

Sister Clare approaches the concept from a different angle: "You know, if everybody's place in life is ultimately a matter of luck, then our goal should be to *protect the unlucky from the scourge of the lucky.*"

"Protect the unlucky from the scourge of the lucky" repeats Una. "I like that!"

"I do too" says Zero "but we need to find an easier way to organize all of this. Every meeting we introduce more and more prescriptions and proscriptions:

DON'T use words like 'hero' or 'villain',

DO protect the unlucky from the scourge of the lucky,

DON'T use words like 'guilty' or 'innocent' or 'good' or 'evil',

DO accept multiple truths,

DON'T make any Fundamental Attribution Errors,

DON'T discuss determinism unless it's necessary for illumination... Soon we're going to have so many of these dicta that we won't be able to remember them all. Determinism shines on every part of our lives. We can't list every part of our lives."

Everybody softly voices concurrence.

Zero continues: "So I propose that we condense everything into a few basic tenets. As I see it, the big thing that determinism shows us is that people are ultimately not responsible for their actions. It's just a matter of luck how people end up. And so we need a different ethics - an enlightened ethics - to help us deal with this. We need a different ethics based on our understanding that everything is luck."

"An Ethics of Luck" I suggest.

"Yes, some kind of Ethics of Luck" continues Zero. "I know we can't be totally true to determinism. We can't hold people totally unaccountable for their violent and destructive behavior. But by following an Ethics of Luck we can at least try to live our lives in a more enlightened way."

We discuss our new "Ethics of Luck" for quite a while. Eventually Una gathers together Twimfina's drawing supplies, and we all get up and head off to the Royal Brice. Twimfina climbs atop Coach's shoulders and enjoys a free ride all the way to the restaurant.

In the Fountain Room there's a surprise for us. Instead of hot chocolate, we're all given chocolate malts with our cookies! It's just perfect for this warm day. Twimfina loves her malt and cookies. Sitting high on her booster seat, she looks like a little Buddha, so calm and knowing.

It's Zero's turn to give the presentation, but he wants to postpone it to next week so that we can continue talking about our all-important Ethics of Luck. With our tall glasses empty and with Twimfina busy drawing, we continue discussing our Ethics of Luck late into the afternoon.

18. Machinists Union Meets in the Library

⚙

June. Several from our group voice "Oo!" with pleasure as we walk into the hallowed St. Louis Public Library and feel the cool air. But my voice isn't among them. Unless it's sticky-humid with mosquitos flying around, I don't care much for air conditioning. I dream about summer heat all winter long. Now that summer's here - or at least it will be in four days - I intend to enjoy the heat as much as I can.

It's Fathers Day and we pass several special displays about fathers as we walk downstairs to our meeting room. There are three meeting rooms downstairs. We've reserved the smallest room on the left.

Walking into the room, my first impression is not a positive one. It has none of the character of Una's loft. It's just a boxy, functional, generic room with fluorescent lighting and a dozen plastic folding chairs arranged in two neat rows facing a small stage area in front. It's only saving grace is that one of the hopper windows along the top of the basement wall was left open, allowing a wonderful, warm, fragrant breeze to waft in from the outside flower garden above us.

"June is bustin' out all over" sings Sister Clare as she smells the honeylike sweetness rolling down from the Butterfly Bush.

"Why don't we make a circle so we don't get lost" suggests Coach. We all chuckle and proceed to arrange the chairs into a circle.

Just then the large bells from the Church of the Free Will across the street start ringing loudly, announcing the noon hour. Coach shouts above the clamor: "Oh no! We forgot to bring Una's alarm clock!"

When the ringing stops, we all sit down and blankly look at each other.

"Well, what do we talk about?" asks Zero.

"Una's not here - we could always talk about her!" jokes Coach. We all laugh.

"Might as well start with the Secretary's Report" I suggest as I open my notebook. "We left off talking about our Ethics of Luck. We described it as a kind of gold standard for determinists to which we could aspire."

"An *unwritten* gold standard" adds Sister Clare.

"Yes" I confirm "we decided to keep our Ethics of Luck unwritten - a book with countless chapters but no words."

"One of those chapters that I'd like to talk about today is the chapter on violence" begins Zero. "We all understand that no behavior is ever truly free. So it follows that any violent response to that behavior is not truly fair. It's really important that we all renounce violence - any kind of violence that causes suffering."

"And those who don't agree, we can beat them up" quips Coach. Everybody chuckles.

"It kind of feels like we're back in EP101 with our Professor, doesn't it?" observes Sister Clare. "He always had this kind of 'Love Your Neighbor' ambiance going on."

"I miss the old guy" says Coach. We all agree - even B.B. who never met him.

Zero stresses his point again: "Nonviolence has got to be the central tenet of our Ethics of Luck. Inflicting suffering on others for any reason is unfair. And I'm not just talking about violence between individuals. The way we treat prisoners is unfair, the way we use our military is unfair, the way we make and sell weapons is unfair... *all* the violent things we do are unfair."

"In other words we should be pacifists" says Sister Clare.

"Absolutely! That's what our Ethics of Luck would expect from us" replies Zero. "We should all be pacifists."

"But I personally don't want to be the kind of pacifist who just sits on his hands and complains" declares Coach.

"Me neither" agrees Zero. "We need to be *active* pacifists - pacifists who actually fix things! I mean we *know* how to do it! We *know* our psychology, we *know* our memetics, we *know* the nuts-and-bolts mechanics of how to change people without using violence."

"We're machinists - we can fix anything!" I respond.

"Right! We're machinists - we can fix anything!" repeats Zero.

"Hey, I like that!" says Coach. "We're machinists - we can fix anything. Maybe we should call ourselves 'Machinists' instead of 'Darwinians.'"

Coming from Coach, this suggestion holds extra weight because he's the one who had originally proposed the name 'Darwinians' back in January. It had been *his* baby. Zero likes the idea too. We only discuss it for a couple of minutes before we agree to call ourselves 'Machinists' and to call our group the 'Machinists Union'. Since St. Louis already has other machinists unions – the real kind – we decide to make our name unique by adding our zip code prefix to it. So our new official name is 'Machinists Union #631'.

I look at the front cover of my notebook and sigh at the 'Darwinians' title that I had spent so much time drawing so carefully. Then I remember and shout: "Una's banner!"

Everybody tries to not laugh. "She's gonna kill us" somebody blurts out. "Who's gonna tell her that we changed our name?" asks somebody else.

"She'll hear about it in next month's Secretary's Report" quips Coach. Everybody laughs.

After a while we all take the comparatively short walk over to the Royal Brice, which is only half as far as it was from Una's. Once there, we all sit around the Fountain Room's mahogany conference table and enjoy our cookies and chocolate malts.

It's Zero's turn to give the presentation, so he quickly finishes his snacks and then begins to pass out stapled handouts to each of us.

On the cover page of the handout is the title: "The Brain Chemistry of Stress and Aggression". None of us are surprised to read this. For as long as we've known him, Zero has had an interest in criminal psychology.

Zero gives an interesting presentation. We talk about 'antisocial personality disorder (ASPD)' and 'psychopathy'. He even has us play around with the 'Hare Psychopathy Checklist' to see if we are psychopaths. Surprisingly, none of us are.

Here we sit, this strange family of ours, sipping malts, talking about testosterone and corticosterone, and having no clue to where all of this is heading.

19. B.B.Brice - Beans & Rice

✿

When Una and Twimfina get back from California, Una calls and suggests that we have our July meeting in the library because it's so hot in her brick loft. Although I actually love the heat and love her brick loft, I go ahead and reserve the same meeting room that we used last month.

On the Sunday of our meeting it's so hot and humid in St. Louis that even I find some relief in walking through the library doors. It also feels good to have all six of us together again - seven counting Twimfina. She's as cute as ever, carrying her "Flower of Life" coloring book and a container of crayons.

When we get downstairs to the meeting room, we arrange our chairs in a circle at the back half of the room like last time. Twimfina walks up front to the stage and places her coloring book on a plastic table.

The bells from the Church of the Free Will across the street start ringing loudly.

"This is great!" marvels Una. "It's warm in the winter, cool in the summer, and we don't even need an alarm clock! We should meet here *every* month!"

"I much prefer your place" I say as persuasively as I can, although nobody seems to hear me.

"Zero, what's the latest with Corky?" asks Sister Clare.

"Yesterday when I saw him, he seemed pretty normal" Zero answers.

"Then the operation cured his libido problem?"

"I didn't ask him, but I really doubt it" he answers. "I don't know much about Kluver-Bucy Syndrome, but I don't see how surgery could possibly make anything better. Worse maybe, but not better. Don't forget that the purpose of the operation was to remove the tumor he had growing in his brain. The surgeons were working to save Corky's life, not deal with his libido. However I must say that he sure looked good and acted normal yesterday. Maybe they have him on some anti-androgen drug or something."

"Well, we better get to work" says Una with a bit of urgency in her voice. Then she cheerfully greets us with her usual: "Welcome to the 9th meeting of the Darwinians."

There's an outburst of laughter from all of us. Una looks puzzled, but continues unabated. "Secretary Michael, where did we leave off?"

I glance at my notebook and reply: "At our last meeting, the Machinists agreed to be *active* pacifists - pacifists who get things done."

"The Machinists?" interrupts Una with some irritation in her voice. "What are you talking about? Who are the Machinists?"

There's some stifled laughter. "You changed our name?" asks Una pointedly with disbelief on her face. "You changed our name without even asking me? And why such a pedestrian name like "Machinists"? What does *that* have to do with our mission?"

"It has everything to do with our mission, Una" says Zero in his most disarming voice. "As we're learning more and more about the social mechanics that make people tick, we're more and more able to repair social inequities that we find. As we get the tools, we should use them."

"Tools to protect the unlucky from the scourge of the lucky" adds Clare.

The more we talk, the less resistance Una puts up. Eventually she seems to accept our new name - begrudgingly perhaps - but she accepts it nonetheless. I'm happy that things are back to normal.

We spend the rest of our time discussing the Ethics of Luck and our commitment to active pacifism. What does it mean to be an active pacifist? What should be the goal of our activism? What are the best tools to use to achieve this goal?

Eventually we put the chairs back into rows and head off towards the Royal Brice. On the way to the restaurant I notice that B.B. has lost a lot of weight. When we first met him a year ago, he was a bit on the chubby side. I remember how he had to squeeze through the narrow doorway as he carried that big tray of cookies into the Fountain Room for us to enjoy. I remember thinking to myself "this fellow's been sampling too many cookies!" But today he looks more like a marathon runner than a cookie sampler.

What happened?

Actually, I'm pretty sure I know what happened. It's Clare. He's fallen under the influence of Clare.

Sister Clare is one of the most persuasive people I've ever met. When she speaks so rationally with her calm, soothing voice, everybody listens. I can't explain why – some people just have that power. Sometimes when I'm at home giving a presidential address in front of the mirror, I try to conduct myself as if I were Clare. I try to maintain her composure and even move my hands in the gentle, reassuring way that she does when making a point. If only I could do that in real life!

Then, as if he had been reading my mind, B.B. asks: "Has anybody noticed that I've lost some weight?"

"You really look good, B.B." we answer - (which is probably the safest way to answer that kind of question).

"Sister Clare has turned me into a vegetarian!" he proudly announces.

"Aha! I knew it!" I think to myself.

"And she's turned the rest of us into vegetables" quips Coach. Everybody laughs. But B.B. keeps on talking about his magical diet.

"Plus I cut out all fat, salt and dairy from my food" he continues. "It's the smartest thing I've ever done."

New converts to anything can be quite entertaining. They often have a special need to share their newly found 'Meaning of Life' with everybody they meet. B.B. is no exception.

"Brothers and sisters, I've been experimenting with different 'bean and rice' recipes" he tells us. "When we get to the restaurant I'd like all of you to give one of the dishes a taste-test."

"Sure!" we answer with enthusiasm.

"I know you all liked the snacks, but this is so much better for your bodies" he adds.

My heart sinks, as I'm sure everybody else's does too. Although nobody says anything aloud, I'm sure everybody is screaming inside: "What?! No more cookies?! No more malts?! And of all things *beans* are taking their place?!"

"Sister Clare and I are planning to launch a new business with these bean and rice dishes" he explains. "Our pledge is that

69

'good nutrition' will always take precedence over everything else
- even 'flavor'. The only two items on the menu will be 'beans'
and 'rice'. We won't charge much for the food and we'll prepare it
without adding any salt or fat. The customer simply chooses one
type of bean and one type of rice. The chosen beans will then be
spooned over the chosen rice in one bowl. There's nothing else.
No meat, no chips, no dairy products, no french-fries, no pastries,
no sodas..."

"No customers..." interjects Coach. We all explode with
laughter, freeing ourselves of any disappointment we had been feeling.

"Does this mean you're going to build your own restaurant?"
I ask as we arrive at the Royal Brice.

"I already have, Brother Michael!" he replies. "Food Carts –
four of them."

"Four food carts?" we echo in surprise.

"We made agreements to provide food at four different colleges, so we ordered four carts. Actually one of them has already
arrived. It's out back next to the loading dock. Wanna see it?"

"Sure!" we reply.

All of us then follow B.B. as he cuts through the kitchen and
winds back through the storage area and past the trash dumpsters,
ending up at the loading dock. "This is the scenic route" he jokes.
As he opens the back door we see it right away: a new white food
cart with the name "B.B.Brice – Beans & Rice" spelled-out in large
letters.

"B.B.Brice – Beans & Rice" reads Una. "That's a nice, mod-
est name. Where'd you get it?" We all laugh.

B.B. blushes as he explains: "It just made good business
sense, Sister Una. My family spent years establishing the 'Royal
Brice' name, so why not capitalize on it? Plus I feel there's a catchi-
ness to it with its rhyme and alliteration. Believe me, it was just
a practical business decision. I have no desire to see my name in
lights."

"Yeah, sure" we reply sarcastically. (Actually, we completely
believe him – we just enjoy watching him squirm a little.)

We all get a tour of the cart and find it relatively comfortable – at least as far as food carts go. It's large enough to allow the

server to move around and ladle-out the food without feeling too cramped. It's insulated to help keep *in* the heat on wintry days, and it has a quiet, solar-powered exhaust fan to help keep *out* the heat and humidity on summer days. It's easy to keep clean inside and out. And on its window it proudly displays a 'Certificate of Sanitation' sticker that the St. Louis Health Department issues.

B.B. had the trailer custom-converted to meet the special needs of a 'Beans and Rice' business. On the inside it has a large, stainless-steel hot-water bath bolted safely to the back wall and the floor. This bath is designed to keep two pots of rice and three pots of beans at a safe temperature of 135°.

On the outside of the cart is a place to post which bean dishes and which rice dishes are available – and a place to list the exact ingredients used (so customers can try out the recipes at home).

Also on the outside of the cart there's a money-box that hangs underneath the window where the customers will pay for their food. On top of the money box is a clear plastic tray with a lever and a trap door. B.B. designed this contraption so that the server would never have to handle any money. Not only does this removable money box help maintain good sanitation, it reduces danger to the worker if there were ever a robbery. The only drawback is that the customers must either have exact change or must use prepaid meal tickets.

"Will you actually cook the food in the carts or just serve it?" asks Zero.

"Just serve it, Brother Zero" replies B.B. "It takes lots of time and heat energy to cook beans. Plus, as you can see, there's not much room in the carts to safely prepare food. So we'll have to cook everything here in our commercial kitchen the night before. We'll use large pressure cookers for the beans. Then in the morning we'll truck the freshly prepared food out to the Campus Carts.

"School starts in about five weeks. Do you think you'll be ready in time?" asks Coach.

"We don't have much choice in the matter, Brother Coach!" chuckles B.B. with some trepidation in his voice. We're under contract! On Tuesday the 29th, we've *got* to be ready! It'll be tight, especially now that Sister Clare has that gig at Channel 2 News, but I think we'll be ready. By the way, will any of you be needing a part-time job this semester?"

"Sure!" we shout.

After B.B. describes the job openings, we walk back to the Fountain Room. Once there, we seat ourselves around the conference table. Sister Clare gives each of us a spoon and a small white bowl. She then places a serving bowl of rice on the table while B.B. brings out three serving bowls of Vegetarian Chili labeled A, B, and C. Our job is to taste-test the different recipes and fill out an evaluation card. Since B.B. isn't using any fat or salt in the dishes, he has to experiment with different spice combinations. We're the guinea pigs - the happy guinea pigs - helping him determine which spices taste the best. All of us find this task to be fun - maybe not as much fun as malts and cookies would have been - but fun nonetheless.

After we finish filling out our evaluation cards and cleaning off the table, it's time for our presentation. This month it's Coach's turn.

Coach describes a study that seems to confirm determinism! The experiment measured brain waves as people performed certain motor tasks, such as pushing buttons. If a subject chooses to press a red button, one would expect that the 'decision' part of his or her brain would light-up before the 'motor' part of the brain lights-up. But in this study, just the opposite happened! The motor part of the brain lit-up before the decision part! This seems to be incompatible with free-will.

It was a short presentation, but we loved it. It was the perfect grist for our mills, the validation we so much needed.

"The science is finally catching up to us!" somebody jokes. We all feel comforted, vindicated, validated, reassured. For a good twenty minutes we are all happy to be determinists.

20. Our Professor

August. The huge bells from the Church of the Free Will have just finished ringing, but their vibrations still hum in the library's downstairs meeting room.

"Welcome to the 10th meeting of the *Machinists Union*" announces Una with a slow, low-pitched, very sarcastic pronunciation of the words 'Machinists Union'. We all chuckle a little. "Secretary Michael, where did we leave off?" she asks.

As I open my notebook, there's a soft tap-tap-tap on our door jamb. We look over and see an elderly man with a gray beard standing in the doorway. At first I kind of assumed it was a homeless man.

"Is this a meeting of the Darwinians?" he asks. (On the schedule posted upstairs, we're still listed as the Darwinians.)

B.B. answers "Yes sir!"

But the rest of us stand up with incredulity as Coach asks: "Professor?"

The old man freezes with a 'deer in the headlights' expression on his face. We all rush forward, knocking over a couple chairs in the process.

"I'm Una" she says as she takes his hand and holds it with both of hers.

"Una!" he repeats with a longing smile.

"I'm Michael"

"Michael!"

"I'm Coach"

"Coach! And lovely Clare! And Zero! Oh, my whole A-Team's here!"

There's a joyful feeling of celebration in the room, as if our long lost grandfather had found his way home.

"Here, we want you to meet the new guy!" says Clare as she ushers B.B. over to our Professor.

"I'm so pleased to finally get to meet you, Professor. My name's B.B.

"I'm happy to meet you, B.B." replies our Professor as he shakes B.B's hand.

Then curious Twimfina, not wanting to miss out on the excitement, walks back to our group, carrying her coloring book.

"And this is the star of our show!" announces Coach as he lifts up Twimfina and sets her down in front of our Professor. "This is Una's daughter Twimfina."

"Twimfina?" asks our Professor, unsure of the pronunciation. We nod. "Twimfina" he repeats as he takes her little hand and kneels down in front of her as if receiving a princess. He turns to Una and adds: "I didn't even know you had a child, Una."

Without understanding the emotional landscape, B.B. explains: "Her biological mother was Purity."

Still holding Twimfina's hand, our Professor's smile of joy turns into a smile of grief. "I'm so sorry, Twimfina" he whispers.

Coach gently pulls Twimfina away and kneels down in her place. "It's okay, buddy" he says as he puts his hand on the old man's shoulder.

Our Professor collapses back, sitting on his legs. Tears well in his eyes. "I'm so sorry" he softly cries. The rest of us try to comfort him. With our hands on his shoulder and back, we repeat over and over "It's okay, Professor. It wasn't your fault."

"She was my student" he sobs.

"It's okay, Professor" repeats Una soothingly.

As the anguished man quietly weeps, Twimfina squeezes between us and puts her little hand on our Professor's shoulder next to her mother's. "It's okay, Professor" she says.

21. Enemia

September. I heard the news while driving to the library. I feel sick that the United States is bombing Enemia. I thought we had outgrown that sort of behavior.

The big bells from the steeple across the street are ringing as I enter the library's downstairs meeting room. I feel a bit embarrassed because usually I'm much earlier than this. Nonetheless everybody greets me as I walk over to the empty chair they've saved for me at my usual place in the circle between Una and Zero. Among those who greet me is our dear Professor. If it weren't for the bombing, this would be a perfect day.

"Welcome to the eleventh meeting of the Machinists Union" announces Una (this time without grotesquely drawing out the 'Machinists Union' vowels). "And before we get started, let's welcome our Professor and express how honored we are to have him as part of our group."

We all cheer for our Professor. I even notice little Twimfina up at the front of the room clapping for him. Our Professor seems a little embarrassed, but he smiles.

"Even though there's breaking news happening in Enemia, we should probably get to work" says Una with a weariness in her voice.

"Or we could just go home and listen to the news" I suggest.

"Do you all want to do that?" Una asks. Nobody answers for a few moments.

"No, let's *not* do that" replies our Professor with certainty in his voice. "I know it's exciting to listen to the radio and to get caught-up in the narrative. And I know there's something satisfying in labeling the fighters as a bunch of Neanderthals. But that's not what active pacifists do. Active pacifists don't listen to the radio. Active pacifists *are* the radio."

It's surprising how one person - one admired person - can sway so many others. It's not that he's changing our minds or persuading us of anything. We're already there. After all, we wrote the book on the Ethics of Luck. It's just that he woke us up again. Waking up can be something big. Mountains wake up from time to time.

"I totally agree with our Professor" says Zero. "This bombing is happening on our watch. We've got to deal with it."

"I don't know" says Coach with some despondency. "I've been following this pretty closely. Believe me, it's a mess - it's an intractable mess.

"We're Machinists – we can fix anything!" I reply with my crowd-pleasing line. The others chuckle and repeat this favorite motto of ours.

"We need to look at this analytically, like any machinist would" says Zero. "We've got to figure out what went wrong. We've got to figure out what the telltale signs were that could have alerted us that things were going wrong. We've got to figure out what we could have done back then to avert this mechanical failure."

"Remember in class how we used to go backwards in time to discover why famous and infamous people ended-up the way they did?" asks our Professor.

"Lives in Reverse!" I interject.

"Yes, Lives in Reverse" he continues with a chuckle. "Why don't we do the same thing here. Why don't we go backwards in time and try to discover how this all started."

"For the source of the problem in Enemia, we'd probably have to go back eons" replies Coach. "The Purist and Heretic groups there have been fighting forever."

After a long pause, Sister Clare responds: "Groups. I think that's the operative word. I have no idea who the 'Purists' or the 'Heretics' are in Enemia - or anywhere else for that matter. And it probably doesn't make any difference. They're just 'fill-in-the-blank' names. It's the word 'groups' that says it all. Zero asked us to find a telltale sign that can alert us when the machinery is heading for failure. I think that we can identify that sign as 'unnecessary grouping'. Unnecessary grouping always seems to be the first step to social disaster - 'Step One' down the Genocide Slide."

There's something exhilarating in hearing Sister Clare speak. She's more reticent than most of us, but when she does say something it's usually worth listening to.

We spent quite some time analyzing how groups get into conflicts. Sister Clare had identified 'Step One'. We went on to identify three more steps. (*We refer to this work as the "Genocide Slide". I will put the full text in the appendix to this book.*)

Although we were pleased with our Genocide Slide document, we wanted to do something with our bodies. We wanted to do something as active pacifists to protest the bombing of Enemia. We discussed it for a few minutes and then decided to hold a half-hour Peace Vigil this evening starting at 7:00.

I ran across the street to make sure that Pastor Causasui had no objections to us standing on the steps of the Church of the Free Will. B.B.Brice offered to bring battery-powered candles for us to hold (sunset is as 7:07 tonight). Sister Clare, who works as one of the 'Roving Reporters' for Channel 2 News, said she'd try to get a video technician to film the event. Una, our artist-in-residence, offered to make signs for us to hold.

Most people would probably consider a peace vigil to be a rather lame response to a bombing raid. We talked about that. But after analyzing it we came to the exact opposite conclusion. We decided that a peaceful, public display of opposition is an important first step to social change. It changes the climate and empowers others to express their disapproval too.

It's 6:45 and all of us but Sister Clare are here on the steps, getting ready for our Peace Vigil. We have a few guests that have come to join us. Coach's father is here, and Pastor Causasui has just walked over from the rectory. She's chatting with our Professor. And Una's roommate Daifu has come to join us too.

This is a great place to stand, here in the heart of St. Louis's cultural district. The streets are packed with cars inching their way to and from Powell Symphony Hall, Fox Theatre, the Sheldon Concert Hall, and all the other museum and art venues that are packed into this area. It's like we have a captive audience!

As Coach tries to arrange us on the steps, I'm trying to tune this old guitar that I have slung over my neck. B.B. is handing out the candles while Zero follows behind, fiddling with the batteries until the temperamental candles light-up. Una is distributing simple, easy-to-read signs for everybody to display. Some signs have the word 'Peace'. Mine has the phrase 'War Has No Victory'. Little Twimfina has made her own sign. I can't quite tell what she's drawn. It looks like a porcupine.

At 7:00 we lift our signs and begin our chant:

Bombing is a Bad Idea!
We want Peace in Enemia!
Bombing is a Bad Idea!
We want Peace in Enemia!

I glance down the street and see Sister Clare on the sidewalk walking this way with her video technician. I nudge Coach who is standing next to me.

"It's show-time" he replies.

As Sister Clare approaches she is talking into her microphone while her technician is focusing her camera on us. When she arrives we stop our singing and chanting. Sister Clare turns directly to Una, just as we had rehearsed.

"Hello, my name's Clare from Channel 2 News. May I ask why you're all demonstrating here?"

"We're here to protest today's bombing of Enemia" replies Una. "We feel the violence is unnecessary and we've come to voice our disapproval."

"You must be very organized to be out here so quickly! Are you a political group or maybe a church group?"

"No, we're science students."

"Science students? Well, *that's* unexpected. What does science have to do with your protest?"

"Well, science helps us see the hidden machinery that connects everybody and everything."

"What hidden machinery?" asks Sister Clare as she moves her microphone back and forth.

"For example, we're in America" begins Una. "Most of us were simply born here. They're in Enemia. Most of them were simply born there. It's just luck where we ended-up. We could just as easily have been born there. They could just as easily have been born here.

"In which case they'd be bombing *us* right now" adds Clare. "Exactly! They'd be bombing us" repeats Una. "Do unto others as you would have them do unto you. *That's* what science teaches us – and *that's* why we're standing out here and that's why we'll *continue* to stand out here every week at this time until this cruelty ends. Clare, you seem like an enlightened, intelligent person. Why don't you join us?"

"I was just thinking the same thing. I've always been a pacifist and I do love science."

"Then you should join us for sure! We call ourselves "Machinists" because we see the world as a machine - a fixable machine. We meet in the library at noon on the third Sunday of every month. Our next meeting will be on October 15th."

"October the 15th at noon?" repeats Sister Clare. "Okay, I'll be there! And you say you'll be demonstrating here on the steps again next week?"

"Absolutely! We plan to hold a half-hour vigil here every Sunday evening until the violence in Enemia stops."

"Even if it takes a long, long time?"

"Well Clare, sometimes nonviolence *takes* a long, long time – but it always gets the job done."

This is my cue to strum a few chords so that we all can begin singing together:

Nonviolence takes a long, long time.
Nonviolence takes a long, long time.
It takes a long, long, long, long, long, long time.
It takes a long, long, long, long, long, long time.

As we sing it over and over, the video technician slowly pans her camera over each of us. (I bite my cheek trying not to burst out laughing when she focuses her camera on me.) I see Sister Clare speaking some final words into her microphone. She then slips the recorder into her shoulder bag and winks at us. Mission accomplished.

Nonviolence Takes a Long, Long Time

Peacefully ♩ = 52   Secretary Michael

Non - vi - o - lence____ takes a long, long time.__ Non - vi - o lence____ takes a long, long time. It takes a long, long, long, long, long, long time. It takes a long, long, long, long, long, long time.____

22. Changing People Without Violence

✿

October. I walk into the library's downstairs meeting room and wonder for a moment if I'm in the right place. All these people! Then I spot Una and a couple of the others welcoming our new guests. Little Twimfina is up in front by herself, drawing. I take a quick head count and come up with seventeen people! Some I recognize from our weekly Peace Vigils, but most are total strangers. They must have seen us on the Channel 2 News last month. "The power of television!" I think to myself.

Just then the big church bells start ringing in the belfry across the street. I sneak across the hall to borrow five folding chairs from an unoccupied room. With ten new people, we've more than doubled in size!

When the ringing stops, Una waits for us to finish arranging the chairs in a circle. It's more of an oval than a circle, but it'll do.

"Welcome to the 12th meeting of the Machinists Union" she finally announces with a smile. "And a special warm welcome to all of you who are here for the first time." (We oldies all briefly applaud the newbies.)

"Before we get started, why don't we all introduce ourselves" she suggests. And that's what we do. Una is the first to introduce herself, followed by Sister Clare and then on around the circle clockwise, ending with me. It's exciting to have such a diverse group of all ages and so many different backgrounds.

"Those of you here for the first time probably learned about us from the Channel 2 News broadcast" begins Una. "So to start things off on the right foot, we need to come clean about something." She puts her hand on Sister Clare's shoulder. "You all recognize my good friend Clare. She's the reporter who interviewed me on TV. We made it seem like we had never met before. But in reality Clare has been with us from the beginning. That interview was completely staged. We had rehearsed it many times."

"We forgive you!" a newbie shouts. Everybody laughs.

Zero chimes in: "Another thing we should make clear is

that we're not a protest group per se. We're science students who happen to share an understanding that there's no free will. Our weekly Peace Vigil is just one of many things we do to be true to that understanding. It's just one of many things we do to live out our mission, which is to help protect the unlucky from the scourge of the lucky."

"You're all determinists?" asks a newbie.

Coach jokes: "Please don't run out the door! We only talk about determinism when we have to!" Everybody laughs.

We then tell the newbies all about our group. In addition to our mission to protect the unlucky from the scourge of the lucky, we tell them about our Ethics of Luck, our Vow of Nonviolence, our Motto (*We're Machinists - We Can Fix Anything!*), our Lasagna Lesson (*the Acceptance of Multiple Truths*), and our newest creation, the Genocide Slide. However we say nothing about the seminal event that brought us all together in the first place - Purity's suicide. With our Professor looking so happy and enjoying everybody's company, we don't dare even mention it.

"Before we head off to the Royal Brice, don't forget about our Peace Vigil tonight on the church steps" Una reminds us.

"The candles should look good tonight because sunset's at 6:20. But next week they should look even better because daylight savings time will be over. It'll be pitch black."

After a few more minutes of miscellaneous this-and-that business, we rearrange our chairs back into neat rows and leave for the Royal Brice Steakhouse.

When we get to the Fountain Room, the newbies express the same wonder as we did when we first stepped into the room. Sister Clare once again brings out a stack of small bowls, some spoons, and a large bowl of rice. Then B.B. once again brings out three serving bowls labeled A, B and C. Today's dish is called 'Red Bean Tangerine'.

Of all the dishes we've evaluated so far, I think this is my favorite. But I find it hard to fill-out my evaluation card because all three bowls taste pretty-much the same. I sure like them, though. Everybody does. There are bits of tangerine skin cooked in with the beans, giving the dish a fresh, unexpected sweetness.

This month it's Una's turn to give the presentation. As she

gets her material together, B.B. cleans off the table. Then Sister Clare, much to our delight, brings out mugs of hot chocolate for us again! With B.B.'s new health kick, I was afraid they were gone forever.

Coach reprises his whine: "Oh Miss? I didn't get as much whipped cream as Michael did!" Everybody laughs again.

Una's presentation is about a book she recently read. The name of the book is 'The Meme Machine' by Susan Blackmore. Just like last time, Una has us transfixed. She is well into her presentation when one of the newbies interrupts and asks her to clarify what a meme is.

"I'm sorry, I should have made that clear at the beginning" she replies. "We're defining a meme as something that can be easily mimicked by others. It could be a word, a way of walking, a facial expression, a melody - almost anything!" She then turns around and calls up to her daughter at the front of the room. "Hey Twimfina, what's that chant we always shout at our Peace Vigil?"

With a steady beat, Twimfina loudly sings "Bombing is a bad idea! We want peace in Enemia!"

Una turns back to the newbie and says "That's a meme - a good one." She then continues with her presentation.

When Una reaches the end, she does something different. Instead of taking questions, she says: "Now let's apply what we've just learned. Our mission is to stand up for the *unlucky* people. That means we're going to need some way to change the *lucky* people. I propose that we do it with fountain-flushes."

"What's a fountain-flush?" we ask.

"It's a sure way of changing people without violence" she answers. "We'll need to form two groups of actors. One group we'll call the **Fountains**. The 'Fountains' are the attractive ones - the ones who must always appear happy, friendly, and educated."

"You mean I have to do this all by myself?" asks a cheeky newbie. We all laugh.

Una continues. "The other group we'll call the **Flushes**. The 'Flushes' are the repulsive ones - the ones who must always appear crude, hostile, and uneducated."

"The attractive Fountains will model the behavior we want to *promote*. The repulsive Flushes will model the behavior we want to *extinguish*. It's pure Memetics! And if you're not yet into memes, consider it pure Psychology - straight from Psych 101!"

"I must have missed that class" jokes another newbie. Again there's laughter.

"People always do what attractive people do" explains Una. "Their doings spray out like fountains and get splashed and re-splashed on everyone. Inversely, people *don't* do what repulsive people do. Their doings get sucked out of everyone and get flushed down the sewer."

"So now that you know what we need from the Fountains and what we need from the Flushes, who wants to be a Fountain?" (Almost everybody raises their hand.)

"Wow" says Una. "I'm almost afraid to ask the next question. Who wants to be a Flush?" (Nobody raises their hand.)

"What?" she asks sarcastically. "Nobody wants to appear unfriendly, unhappy, unintelligent, avoided by others...?" (There's silence.)

"I will" sounds a lone voice. All of us oldies are stunned. It's our Professor.

23. Testosterone Theater Fountain-Flush

✿

"Welcome to the 13th meeting of the Machinists Union" announces Una on this brisk windy day in mid-November. "And a happy birthday to us! Our first meeting was a year ago today!" Everybody smiles and makes a few celebratory sounds. We have about twenty in our group today. We've switched to a larger meeting room. Other than being larger, this room is almost identical to the previous one. Same stage area, same chair arrangement, same hopper windows high up along one wall (although the outside fallen leaves are blocking our view).

"Secretary Michael, where did we leave off?" Una asks. I glance down at my notebook and reply: "We left off talking about the fountain-flush. We were discussing how we might use it as a tool for changing people's behavior."

Our Professor interjects: "And I think we might have a need to use our fountain-flush and our other tool, the Genocide Slide, right away."

"Why?" We're all very curious.

"I brought a film with me today that I'm hoping we might watch when we get to the Fountain Room" he begins. (*This sounds pretty good to me. I like movies but probably haven't seen one since Sister Clare showed us the Charles Darwin film back in January.*)

"It's a new film that's scheduled to be released over the holidays" he continues. "It was sent to me by a film critic who used to be a student of mine. He sent it to me because he feels that it might be a 'hate film.'"

Our Professor takes the film cassette out of his satchel and holds it close to his face so he can read the title. "*Enemia – the Heart of Evil*" he reads. "Hmm – doesn't sound like a hate film to me" he says so earnestly. "Sounds more like a nice balanced documentary." We all laugh.

'*Enemia – the Heart of Evil*'. We've all heard of this movie. It's probably the most heavily advertised of the upcoming holiday films. None of us doubt that it will be violent because that's how it's being promoted. I imagine that the film's producers are just elated that the film is being released during this time of conflict.

"As active pacifists, I feel we might have to do a fountain-flush at the movie theater to dissuade people from watching this" predicts our Professor. (*Some of our metal folding chairs squeak a little as we stir uncomfortably.*)

"Whether we do or don't I guess depends on where the movie falls on our Genocide Slide. As you know, **Step 1** of the Slide deals with 'Grouping'. **Step 2** of the Slide deals with 'Negative Speech'. As I see it, the title alone takes us to **Step 2** – the title alone warrants a fountain-flush – the title alone requires some sort of protest. But it may even be worse. We might decide that the film reaches **Step 3** – the level of 'Hate-Speech'. We might even decide that it reaches **Step 4** – the 'Incitement' and 'Fear' level. If that's the case, then you know it becomes our responsibility to somehow block the screening."

Block the screening? Yikes! I think we all felt rather proud of our Genocide Slide when we put it together back in September. But here we are only a couple months later and we find that we might have to actually *implement* the thing! Here we are with the ink hardly dry, finding that we might be facing some sort of confrontation!

We continue talking about it all the way to the Royal Brice. We even talk about it during B.B.'s taste test, which this month is a delicious all-green dish called 'Celery Split-Pea'.

After we clean-off the table and set-up the projector, our Professor seems reluctant to start the movie.

"Assuming this is indeed a hate-film" he warns, "we better prepare ourselves before watching it. After all, we're just as susceptible to these viruses as anybody else." He then asks Zero, a serious student of psychology, for advice on how we might go about immunizing ourselves.

"Well, maybe we could start by trying to guess what we're going to *see* in the movie" suggests Zero. "If we can *anticipate* what's coming, maybe we'll be able to dismiss it before it soaks in. Maybe we'll be able to blunt its shock."

"That seems reasonable" replies our Professor. "Years from now we sure don't want any of these images still floating around in our memories. So let's follow Zero's suggestion. Let's try to predict what we're going to see. Suppose you were a filmmaker yearning for box-office success. Suppose you wanted to cash-in big on the fear that people already have towards Enemia. How would you depict the Enemians to get the most 'bang' for your buck?"

"Depict them as irrational and inhuman" answers a newbie.

"Irrational and inhuman" repeats our Professor. "I think that's exactly it. That's just what we've got to watch-out for. That's the poison. And by the way, 'dehumanization' puts us way down on **Step 3** of our Genocide Slide. That's the step that calls for a public rebuke." (*We all stir uncomfortably again, but these sturdy chairs don't squeak like the library chairs do.*)

Our Professor continues: "And as you watch the film, what feelings should concern you? What feelings should warn you that you're being poisoned?"

"Fear" answers Zero. "And vengeance" he adds.

"Squash them roaches!" shouts a newbie. (*We all chuckle a little, embarrassed at recognizing that feeling.*)

"And what shocking things do you think we'll see to elicit that fear and to bring-on those feelings of vengeance?" asks our Professor.

"Terrorist attacks" suggests a newbie.

"And you can be sure the camera will linger on each man-gled body" adds Zero.

"I don't think I want to see this movie" confesses Sister Clare.

"Then don't watch it" advises our Professor. "Nobody should watch anything they feel will hurt them. I sure won't be watch-ing it. Clare, you can come sit with me and Twimfina over at the fountain and watch the fish instead. They're Oscar fish – really magnificent creatures – and presumably a lot more "Oscar" than this movie will ever be."

We chuckle, not quite sure whether our Professor is seri-ous about not watching the movie. But he affirms it, saying "I'm not joking. I've seen too many of these things in my life. It's not entertainment for me. I don't need it anymore. I don't *want* it anymore."

"But if we decide to do a fountain-flush, will you be with

us?" asks a newbie with a concerned tone in his voice.

"Oh sure. I'll do my job as the Flush. I'll *always* do my job as the Flush. I just don't want to sit through any more hate-movies. That part of my life is over. I don't have the stomach for it anymore. I'm too old and too tired. I want to go out singing. You'll have to watch it and evaluate it without me."

And with that he turns on the projector and walks over to the fountain with Twimfina. B.B. gets up and switches-off the chandelier. For the next couple of hours we watch and comment and take notes. After the film is over, we bring back our Professor and begin planning for our first fountain-flush.

We check the newspaper's movie section and learn that the film is scheduled to be released this Friday, the day after Thanksgiving. It'll be opening at the Testosterone Theater. This is no surprise. Almost all of the loud and violent films open there.

After our meeting, some of us drive over to the Testosterone Theater to check-out the neighborhood. We introduce ourselves to a couple of the adjacent businesses and get permission to meet on their parking lots. We want to make sure that when opening day arrives, we'll be well-prepared, well-rehearsed and ready to roll.

And we are. On opening day at 1:00 in the afternoon, a couple dozen of us Machinists meet near the theater. As 'Fountains' our job is to make a positive impression. And so we're all cleanly dressed, overly polite, and constantly smiling. Each of us holds a 'Stop the Hate' protest sign in one hand and a camera in the other.

Our plan is this: whenever a prospective movie-goer approaches the ticket window, we will spring into action. Coach will start us off by counting: "One, Two, Three, Four!" And then we'll all loudly chant:

"Hate and fear – we've had enough! Only the ignorant like this stuff!
Hate and fear – we've had enough! Only the ignorant like this stuff!
Hate and ignorance – what a mixture!
Come and let us take your picture! CHEESE!"

And then we'll all lift our cameras and snap a picture. The bright unexpected flash of cameras will hopefully freeze the moviegoers in their tracks and cause them to turn around and leave.

About a half hour before the first showing, we begin our performance. Within twenty minutes a large crowd has gathered with none of them daring to approach the ticket booth. The police soon arrive, but we are doing nothing illegal. The flashing lights of the police cars only add to the spectacle.

Standing in front of the theater not too far from us is Sister Clare. Her part-time job as a Roving Reporter for Channel 2 News is giving us lots of exposure. As she faces the News camera, she holds her microphone and describes the scene before her:

"Good afternoon! I'm standing here in front of the Testosterone Theater. It's supposed to be Opening Day for the new film "Enemia – the Heart of Evil", but as you can see there is absolutely nobody in line to buy tickets – nobody!"

As Clare continues, three women approach the theater. They are happily talking amongst themselves and are oblivious to what is going on. Coach counts-off: "One, Two, Three, Four!" And we once again spring into action:

"Hate and fear – we've had enough! Only the ignorant like this stuff!
Hate and fear – we've had enough! Only the ignorant like this stuff!
Hate and ignorance – what a mixture!
Come and let us take your picture! CHEESE!"

And then we all lift our cameras and snap their pictures. The women are startled. One begins laughing and pulls her friends away as they all escape back into the anonymity of the crowd.

"It's easy to understand why nobody's in line" continues Clare. "There's a large protest group here that snaps photos of anybody who even *begins* to approach the ticket window. Let's go over and see if we can get any of the protestors to talk with us."

Clare walks over to us and, as rehearsed, strikes-up a conversation with one of our newbies - a particularly sweet-looking young woman. "Excuse me, may I ask why you're here this afternoon?"

The sweet-looking young woman replies: "My friends and I are here to beg people to please not watch this movie. It's poison. If they watch it, they will poison *themselves*, they will poison *us their community*, and they will poison the people of Enemia. We've seen the movie. It is "hate-speech" pure and simple."

Clare asks: "But don't people have the right to make that decision for themselves?"

The young woman replies: "To eat the festering egg salad to see if they really *do* get sick like everybody else?" She sweetly chuckles then continues: "Yes of course. But most people would appreciate knowing about the egg salad *before* they sat down for lunch. That's why we're here – to warn the innocent picnickers about the slop being served – and to stop those who unscrupulously dish it out." The young woman then notices our Professor approaching. "Oh, somebody's coming! I've got to get back to work!"

Clare thanks her as Coach begins counting-off again: "One, Two, Three, Four!" And then all of us Fountains once again chant:

"Hate and fear – we've had enough! Only the ignorant like this stuff!
Hate and fear – we've had enough! Only the ignorant like this stuff!
Hate and ignorance – what a mixture!
Come and let us take your picture! CHEESE!"

Our Professor turns towards our flashing cameras and waves: "Thank you, kids! Thank you! Hope ya got a good one!" Our Professor looks shockingly bizarre. He appears to have just crawled out of a trash dumpster. What little hair he has sticks out in an oily mess. His baggy clothes are so filthy it's hard to make-out the colors. His torn, laceless shoes flop as he stumbles along. With both hands he cradles a large, grease-stained, brown paper bag.

Clare holds her microphone up to our Professor: "Excuse me, sir. May I ask why you've come to the Testosterone this afternoon?"

"I comes to see that new movie – the one about Enemia! I thinks it's gonna be a dandy – a dandy!"

Clare continues: "You might not have heard, but there are strong objections to the screening of this film. The Post-Dispatch says it's stupid and disgusting. And the protestors over there… (*she points to us*)

"You means the Camera Club?"

"No, they're not a camera club, they're protestors. They call this a "hate-movie". They say it incites hatred against the Enemi-ans."

"Against the Enemians? Oh, that's okay. I pretty-much hates 'em anyways."

With an embarrassed chuckle, Clare presses on: "They also say this movie is full of blood and cruelty."

"Really? Oooo, that's great! I *loves* that kinda stuff!"

Clare half-chuckles again as she continues: "But this is dif-ferent. In fact two organizations have found the movie so offensive they've already filed lawsuits. They want to protect people from seeing scenes of torture and beheadings.

"Ooooo Baby! It's soundin' better and better all the time! Keeps on talkin'! – I's about to wet my pants!"

(*Clare looks defeated as she changes the subject.*) "Is that your lunch in that big bag?"

"Can ya smells it?" (*Our Professor holds the bag up to Clare's nose as she recoils. Our Professor then rests the bag on a trash receptacle and pulls out a large jar which is sealed with a dirty handkerchief attached with a rubber band.*)

"This ain't no ordinary jar of mayonnaise! Huh-uh! There's a *surprise* inside! – lots of surprises! (*Our Professor pulls off the hand-kerchief and sticks his fingers down into the mayonnaise and starts digging around.*)

"Let me see if I can catch myself one of them little fishies. I just *loves* pickled fishies, don't you?" (*He continues digging around in the mayonnaise.*)

"Here fishie! Here fishie! I just *loves* to pop 'em in my mouth while I'm watchin' a movie. Here fishie! Ah! I caughts me a whopper!" (*Our Professor pulls out a fish, dripping in mayonnaise and dangles it in front of the camera.*)

Clare tries to hide her revulsion. "Well, I'm sure you'll want to get inside and watch that movie now!" she says with feigned excitement. "Is there anything you'd like to say to our viewers at home before you go in?"

(*Our Professor looks directly into the camera while he still dangles the fish*) "Ladies and gentlemen, if you're like me, you'll loves this movie! You'll *loves* it!" (*Our Professor then puts the fish back into the mayonnaise and loudly licks and sucks his fingers.*)

"So come on down and sits next to me! We can be friends! I'll even gives you one of my fishies! We can whoops and holler for the good guys to win! We can whoops and holler!" (*Our Professor then blows his nose and wipes his mouth with the handkerchief and carefully reattaches it to the mouth of the jar with a rubber band.*)

"Yep, you and me – we'll haves a *good* ol' time! – a *good* ol' time!

"What in the world has happened to our Professor?" we oldies wonder. During the EP101 days, he was always so proper. Something must have happened to him during the months since then. Some kind of surrender has occurred – some kind of letting-go. Maybe it was the pain of Purity's suicide that somehow short-circuited the 'pride' part of his brain. Because it's gone, baby, it's gone! I think it probably hurts him to play the Flush, but he plays it without complaint. Like a traffic cop standing in an intersection during a howling ice storm, the unpleasant job has to be done. Our Professor gets it done.

24. New Kitchen

✿

December - eight days before Christmas. It snowed yesterday, but the temperature is already in the upper 40's, so it'll probably melt soon. I was the first one here in the library this morning, arriving even before Una and Twimfina. This gave me time to space the chairs out evenly in a nice circle. I also went up to the stage and brought the lectern down here and set it near the door. I put a pencil and paper on it so that everybody can record their name and contact information. I should have done this months ago.

"Good morning, Secretary Michael!" says Una as she walks through the door.

"Good morning, Una!" I reply. I admit that I like the name 'Secretary Michael'. It makes me feel that I have a purpose - a rare feeling for a determinist like me.

"Good morning, Secretary Michael" repeats Twimfina.

"Good morning, Twimfina!" I reply, trying not to laugh.

Soon all the others begin arriving. It's a large group. I had put all 24 chairs in the circle. Now I'm wondering if we'll have enough.

Sister Clare and B.B. come in together. I notice that B.B. looks a bit tired. I'm not surprised. I'm tired too and I predict the others will look tired when they get here. Why? We've been working late hours.

You see, Zero, Coach, Sister Clare and I all work in the new 'B.B.Brice – Beans & Rice' food carts every day. Business is really good at the colleges. Sometimes the students are lined-up for a block to buy the cheap and healthful dishes. Often we have to close early because we run out of food. But that's not the reason we're so tired.

The success of the new business has created some problems. One is that we seem to have caused some friction between our cooks and the regular kitchen staff at the Royal Brice Steakhouse. We have two 'Beans & Rice' cooks who use the Steakhouse kitchen overnight to prepare our pots of beans and rice. They're supposed to clean-up afterwards and return all the cooking tools to their proper places. They almost always do this, but whenever there's the tiniest infraction the Royal Brice chef gets really upset.

The Royal Brice staff also complains that our equipment is taking up space in their storage room. It's true that our new pressure cookers are pretty-much useless for anything on the Steakhouse menu. And they do indeed take-up space, as do our big rice cookers and the extra pots we use. But that's what storage rooms are for!

In addition to these physical problems, there seems to be some metaphysical ones. The Royal Brice Steakhouse has always catered to affluent people. B.B. and the rest of us feel that the new 'Beans & Rice' business should have a presence in depressed areas where fresh fruits and vegetables are scarce and where obesity and diabetes have become public health problems. And don't forget that B.B. is a newly converted vegetarian, so he undoubtedly has misgivings about preparing his 'Beans & Rice' dishes in a steakhouse of all places. So those of us who work with him have long suspected that we'd eventually have to move to a kitchen of our own.

That time has come. Earlier this month B.B. signed a lease for a commercial space down on Franklin Avenue. It's a street-level storefront in an old, six-story building. It's a fairly large space. It should give us enough room for a commercial kitchen as well as room for a small restaurant.

But the place is filthy. The previous lessee – a large pawn shop – had gone belly-up a few years ago. Ever since then it's been vacant. The owner has never been able to attract any other businesses. It's no wonder. There's graffiti on the walls and layers of dirt on the windows. And the mess goes much higher than street-level. The upper five stories operate as a hotel – and they too are a mess.

B.B.'s no dummy when it comes to business matters. He knew that the hotel business was floundering. He knew that the building's owner was desperate to lease the street-level storefront – not just for the income but to stop the property's deterioration. And so from what I understand, B.B. had the leverage to negotiate a contract with very favorable terms.

So to make a short story long, this is the main reason why some of us - and especially B.B. - are so tired. Ever since UMSL's winter break began, we've been working every day late into the night, trying to get the trashed property cleaned-up in time for next semester.

Now, getting back to our December meeting in the library. It was pleasant enough, but there was nothing out of the ordinary to report on. However I will relate something that I found quite beautiful afterwards when we were in the Fountain Room.

It was Coach's turn to give the Presentation. He came with his father and with an old family friend who is staying with them this week. The friend is a retired veterinarian who used to be their neighbor when they were farming in Minnesota. This elderly gentleman gave the Presentation today.

The title of the veterinarian's Presentation is "One Health". It's about the commonality that all creatures share in their need for good health and in their vulnerability to disease. It only takes him a few sentences to draw us into the world of evolutionary medicine.

"What do you call a veterinarian who specializes in one species?" he asks. Since none of us know, he answers the question himself: "A physician." We all laugh at his joke.

Having practiced veterinary medicine for over forty years, he has many interesting stories to tell us about health problems that afflict other animals. The health problems sound very familiar. He tells us about rabbits with uterine cancer, about dogs with prostate and pancreatic cancers, about tigers and jaguars with breast and ovarian cancers, about heart failure and diabetes and depression and STD's and so many other problems that most of us assumed were only human. "Physiology is physiology" he tells us. Like I said, it was a beautiful Presentation.

25. Money

✿

The third Sunday in January is bitterly cold. Even though I have fond memories of our pajama circles, I'm quite happy to be here in the warm library.

There are only fourteen of us waiting for the big noon bells to ring. We oldies are all here, but quite a few newbies haven't shown up yet - probably because of the frigid weather.

Sister Clare and I smile at each other. She looks tired, but not as tired as poor B.B. sitting clockwise next to her. It takes so much work to establish a new restaurant.

We finished cleaning-up our new kitchen and restaurant space well before the start of the winter semester. In fact we've been in business for more than two weeks now - ever since the St. Louis Health Department inspected us and posted an 'A' on our front door.

'B.B.Brice – Beans & Rice' is the clean, bright new kid on the block – the kid who is giving fresh hope to the entire Franklin Avenue neighborhood. The space being rented by B.B. is divided into two separate sections. The smaller section is the commercial kitchen where the beans and rice are prepared for our fleet of Campus Carts. The larger section is a take-out restaurant with a few tables in it.

In some ways the restaurant looks like any other efficient, modern, fast-food place. It has stacks of white bowls, a napkin dispenser, and a cash register on a stainless steel counter. That stainless steel counter was quite expensive. In fact there was some debate about whether or not we should purchase it. I'm happy we did. It looks professional, it's easy to clean, and it just seems to make everything more orderly.

I often catch myself referring to it as 'our' restaurant. On paper of course none of it belongs to me. But I've given so much of myself to its success that I do feel a kind of metaphysical ownership. To a person like me with humble resources, this is the only kind of ownership I'm ever likely to have. Did I mention that I also own the city park and the public library? Yes, I'm quite content with metaphysical ownership.

High on the wall behind our new stainless steel counter is a large menu board on which hang the name-cards of 7 dishes. Today there are 4 bean selections and 3 rice selections from which to choose. Below the menu board sits a hot water bath with 7 large pots in it. When a customer comes into the restaurant, he or she chooses one kind of rice and one kind of bean. The server then takes a white bowl, spoons-in the chosen rice, and then ladles the chosen beans on *top* of the rice. That's it! One bowl and one price. Nothing else. Thirsty? There's a drinking-fountain with pure, award-winning St. Louis water.

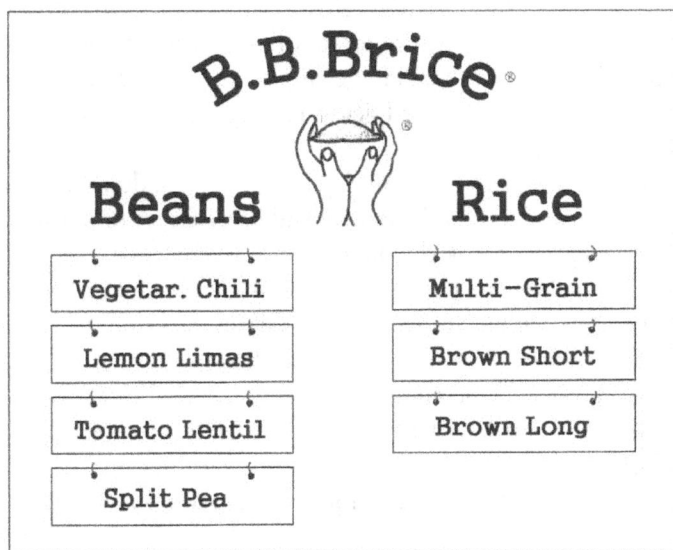

B.B.Brice ®

Beans   Rice

Vegetar. Chili	Multi-Grain
Lemon Limas	Brown Short
Tomato Lentil	Brown Long
Split Pea	

(Menu Board in Restaurant)

That's where I was this past Thursday - in our restaurant - fixing a beat-up piano that the pawn shop abandoned when they went out of business a few years back. It was wise of them to leave it behind. It's an old Lester spinet that's not even playable. All the plastic elbows in its action have disintegrated and crumbled like sugar cookies. I remember thinking "It's going to take hours to fix this thing!"

It had been snowing all day that Thursday. The streets were sloppy with dirty slush. It was a little past closing time. Sister Clare was cleaning-up behind the counter. As usual there were still a few stragglers in the store – street peddlers whom Sister Clare had befriended over the past couple of weeks.

The front door opens and B.B. walks into the restaurant carrying a couple of empty pots that need to be washed. Since I'm on the floor behind the piano, he doesn't notice me. He calls out: "Clare, I'm back!" When Sister Clare greets him, he starts telling her about his rough day. "The Forest Park cart totally ran out of rice. They had to close for about ten minutes."

"Oh no! How'd *that* happen? Were you late?"

"No – in fact I was early! Then the Flo Valley cart ran out of Lemon Limas. And then to top it all off, the Meramec cart got a flat tire. What a fun day! I'm getting some tire tools and a flash-light now to go fix it. I hope I get to lay in the slush. I've always wanted to do that."

Sister Clare laughs. "Fun day here too. Oh, don't forget the trash – I put two bags by the door. And don't forget to put-up the 'CLOSED' sign and lock the door."

"Okay, okay" says B.B. in a comical 'Don't nag me!' voice. B.B. puts up the 'CLOSED' sign and is dragging out the trash bags when a nicely-dressed gentleman approaches.

"Excuse me…" he says.

B.B. pulls the keys from his pocket. "I'm sorry, we're just now closing".

"But I'm not here to eat – I just wanted to talk with the owner."

"Oh, Clare can help you – behind the counter" replies B.B. as he holds the door open for the man.

"Thank you" replies the gentleman as he walks into the res-taurant and over to the counter where Sister Clare is working.

"Clare honey, the janitor said you might be able to help me get in touch with the owner."

"Speaking" replies Sister Clare with a smile.

"*You're* the owner?" asks the gentleman.

Sister Clare smiles as she keeps working. "We're a co-op.

We don't really *have* an owner. But it's my turn to handle business matters, so I guess I'm as close to an owner as you'll get."

"I had *hoped* to talk with B.B.Brice, if that's possible."

Sister Clare chuckles a little. "You already did. He just stepped out."

"Oh! I thought he was the *janitor!*"

"He is. We rotate our jobs."

"Oh. Well then, Clare, I guess it's *you* I should be introducing myself to." He extends his hand and says "I'm Doctor Frank. You've probably heard of me. I own the medical practice in the bank across the street."

Sister Clare shakes his extended hand and replies: "Oh, of course!" She then sings his commercial jingle:

Doc - tor   Frank   of   the   Frank - 'l -in   Bank

"The one and only!" replies the doctor.

Sister Clare chuckles. "I'm happy to meet you, Doctor."

"And I'm delighted to meet you, Clare." Doctor Frank then gets right to the point. "Clare, the reason I wanted to talk with the owner is…"

"Let me guess" she interrupts. "You want to buy our business."

Doctor Frank is surprised. "Wow – I'm glad we're not playing poker!" he says.

Sister Clare laughs a little. "Am I right?"

"Well, yes. We're thinking of building a parking garage. This would be the perfect location."

"A parking garage? How's that even possible? They're not selling the hotel, are they?"

"Well, I've heard some gossip" replies the doctor.

"But we just signed the lease a few weeks ago! We're *definitely* not for sale!" she says with some worry in her voice.

Doctor Frank then speaks very soothingly in his most placating voice. "I know, Clare – I know. I just wanted to let you know that if you ever *did* decide to move onward and upward with your lives, I'd be willing to make a generous offer for your lease – a generous, *generous* offer."

"How generous is 'generous, *generous*'?" she chuckles.

"Well, let's just say that you'd never again have to work in a little soup kitchen – never again!"

Sister Clare smiles at his sales-pitch and says. "But I don't *have* to work in a little soup kitchen *now!*"

At this time, a thin older man enters the restaurant through the fire exit. Sister Clare's tone changes as she speaks to him endearingly in a sing-song voice: "Francis Mendicant, I have your plate ready! I hope you're hungry!"

"Oh, thank you, Clare!" replies the older man. "I owe so much to you and B.B."

"Hey, stop that kind of talk – you owe us nothing" scolds Sister Clare playfully as Mr. Mendicant accepts his treasured container of food and begins to walk back towards the exit.

"Who said there's no free lunch?" jokes Dr. Frank softly.

Sister Clare then calls out to Mr. Mendicant before he reaches the door: "Oh, Francis?"

"Yes, Clare?" he responds as he stops and turns around.

"I'd like to introduce you to Dr. Frank. You probably know his commercial." Sister Clare then sings the jingle: "*Dr. Frank of the Franklin Bank.*"

Mr. Mendicant returns and shakes Dr. Frank's hand. "Oh, I'm happy to meet you, doctor! I'm Francis Mendicant." He then sings different words to the same jingle: "*Francis Mendicant of the City Indigent.*" Mr. Mendicant then laughs heartily at his own joke. Dr. Frank politely laughs also, but with some unease.

"Francis and I are old friends" says Sister Clare with a smile.

Dr. Frank pleasantly jokes: "We sure have good taste in first names, don't we Francis?"

"Yes we do" laughs Mr. Mendicant. "And good taste in restaurants too!" he adds. Both men laugh.

"Well, it was sure nice to meet you, sir!" says Dr. Frank, apparently trying to draw the conversation to a close.

"And you too, Doctor!" replies Francis Mendicant, who then thanks Sister Clare again and exits with his food.

Sister Clare resumes wiping down the counter as Dr. Frank asks: "Clare, how'd you like to go out to dinner with me – someplace where we could discuss this more leisurely. Pick your favorite restaurant – money's no object – it's my treat."

"Oh, that's very tempting! My favorite restaurant. And you're sure that money's no object?"

"Not at all. Just close your eyes and reach for your dream."

Sister Clare closes her eyes, reaches out her hand and then snaps her fingers. "I've *got* it! The place I've been dreaming about for *years!*"

"Yes?" prods Dr. Frank with some excitement in his voice.

"*B.B.Brice – Beans & Rice*" announces Sister Clare dreamily and reverently.

Dr. Frank pauses in resignation. "You know, it's interesting to talk with you, Clare. It's kind of refreshing in a way. Most people treat me much differently because of my – you know – celebrity. But I sure don't get much adulation from you – in fact I don't get any at all!"

Sister Clare laughs a little and says: "Adulation? Of course not – that would be unethical."

"Unethical? How could praying at *my* altar ever be unethical?"

Sister Clare laughs a little. "Because being submissive to people hurts them – turns them into tyrants – makes them ugly."

Dr. Frank flirtatiously replies: "Clare, I'm quite certain that *nothing* could make *you* ugly."

"Oh, it isn't the worship*er* who has to worry" explains Sister Clare. "It's the worship*ee* – the person *receiving* the worship. *That's* the person who has to worry."

"I see" replies Dr. Frank. "Well then, I guess I should thank you for keeping me so handsome."

"You are very welcome, Doctor" chuckles Sister Clare.

After a pause, Dr. Frank returns to the issue of money. "Clare, may I ask how much money you make at this job? Ballpark figure."

"Believe it or not, I really don't know" answers Sister Clare. "I never much think about it. We've pegged our salaries to a 'living wage' index, so it varies. But I'm satisfied.

Dr. Frank loudly exhales in a dismissive sort of way "Living wage index? Poverty."

Sister Clare maintains a pleasant voice while saying: "Well, if this is poverty, then poverty's my privilege."

"Your *privilege*? You call poverty a '*privilege*'? Clare, I don't wish to boast, but I probably make more in one afternoon than you make in an entire *month*. What do you call *that*?"

"Theft?" she asks.

Dr. Frank is taken aback. "Oh, so you're one of '*those*' he says slowly and contemptuously.

Sister Clare laughs a little. "Yes, I guess I *am* one of '*those*' (playfully mimicking his tone of voice).

"Too bad. I never would have guessed you for the jealous type" bemoans the doctor.

Sister Clare laughs a little. "I'm *not* jealous. I just don't feel that doctors should be wealthy. I know it's not very capitalistic of me – but it just doesn't feel right.

"Wow! What a coincidence! I was just about to say the same thing!" exclaims Dr. Frank with exaggerated amazement in his voice.

"Oh, come on" responds Sister Clare with a tone of disbelief.

"No, really, I was! Because I just don't feel that soup kitchen workers should be wealthy. I know it's not very capitalistic of me – but it just doesn't feel right."

Both laugh. "Touché!" concedes Sister Clare, accepting defeat.

The front door rattles as somebody tries to come in. Sister Clare calls out: "Sorry – we're closed!"

Dr. Frank looks at the small group of regulars still sitting around a table, talking. "Doesn't look very closed to me" he says.

"Oh, these *slowpokes* are always the last to leave" replies Sister Clare loudly enough so they can all hear. She comically draws out the word "slowpokes".

The four peddlers sitting around the table hear her and chuckle.

"They like to philosophize with each other after a day on the streets – not that the St. Louis Cardinals have much to do with philosophy" she jokes.

"This place sure seems to be popular" observes Dr. Frank. "I notice at lunchtime the line goes all the way down the street."

"Yeah, we serve *hundreds* for lunch. The Campus Carts do too. In fact recently we've been running out of food."

"Then you need to raise your prices" instructs Dr. Frank.

"Raise our prices? Why?"

"To maximize your profits – supply and demand – simple economics."

"But what if we don't *want* to maximize our profits? What if we want to *minimize* them?"

"Minimize your profits?" Dr. Frank laughs. "Oh yeah – poverty – I forgot."

"*Not*-so-simple economics" teases Sister Clare.

"No, I guess not" replies the doctor. He then looks up at the menu board. "So you serve beans and rice here? How does it all work?"

"Well, you just pick the kind of rice you want and then the kind of beans you want on *top* of the rice" explains Sister Clare. "That's it!"

"That's it?" echoes Dr. Frank. "No drinks? No desserts?"

"Nope. Only sustenance" she answers.

"No wine? No fluffy pastries? Why so ascetic? You have to admit, Clare, a little vice is kind of nice. You might even call it – what's your word – 'sustenance'?"

Sister Clare chuckles a little but says nothing.

Dr Frank looks at the four peddlers who remain in the store. They have their boxes of merchandise next to them as they talk amongst themselves. "Let's see. Who all do we have here? A book peddler?" he asks.

"But not just *any* books" explains Sister Clare. She then shouts over to the book peddler: "James, hold up one of your books, please!" James reaches over to his box and holds up one of his books.

"See how tiny they are?" points out Sister Clare. "He writes them himself. Each one's a story based on some psychological principle. They're really fun to read!"

"Interesting" responds Dr. Frank. "And a fruit peddler?" he asks.

"But not just *any* fruit. He always has something unusual from some far corner of the world. This week it's loquats – one of my favorites!"

"Very interesting!" comments the doctor. "And a hat peddler?"

"But not just *any* hats. He folds them himself out of yesterday's newspaper. He's quite famous. They're really beautiful!"

"Out of newspaper? *That's* different! And who's she – a charity kisser?"

"Now *that* should be right up your alley" teases Sister Clare. "$2 for a kiss. As you said yourself: 'a little vice is kind of nice.'"

(*The peddlers, now done with their dinner, take their bowls and spoons up to the counter for Sister Clare.*) "Thanks Clare. As always, it was great!" says the Charity Kisser.

"Excuse me, Miss Charity Kisser" interrupts the doctor. "Are you still open for business?"

"If your $2 are still open for business" she answers.

Dr. Frank opens his wallet. "Indeed they are!" he says as he pulls out the $2. He then adds a condition: "But only if you would like a little fruit for dessert."

The Kisser looks at the Fruit Peddler and says: "Sure! He has loquats today!"

Dr. Frank then adds another condition: "And only if Mr. Fruit Peddler would like to keep the sun and snow off his head."

The Fruit Peddler looks at the Hat Peddler and says: "You know, my daughter Tangerine is always asking me to bring home one of your hats. She wants to study the folds so she can learn how to make them herself."

Dr. Frank adds one last condition: "And only if Mr. Hat Peddler would like to read a little book tonight."

The Hat Peddler looks at the Book Peddler and says "Sounds good to me! I could *use* some new ideas in my life!"

"Well then, I guess we can do business" says Dr. Frank as he hands the Kisser his $2. She hugs him and kisses him on the cheek. She then turns to the Fruit Peddler and exchanges the $2 for a cup of loquats. The Fruit Peddler then hands the $2 to the Hat Peddler who takes out a newspaper and carefully folds a hat with easy-to-learn folds made especially for Tangerine. The Hat

Peddler then hands the $2 to the Book Peddler and receives a small booklet in return.

"Do you understand now, Clare? A little vice *is* kind of nice!" concludes Dr. Frank with a bit of personal triumph in his voice.

"Well…" says Sister Clare rather dubiously.

"Excuse me – the lesson has not been learned" announces Dr. Frank loudly to the peddlers. "Let's try it again. Would you please give back the book? The hat? The fruit?" The entire chain reverses itself. As Dr. Frank receives the $2 back from the Kisser, he kisses her and says "I guess I better give you your kiss back."

"Now, let's try it again. And pay close attention this time, Clare" says the doctor in his most professorial voice. The entire chain is repeated as he describes each step. Afterwards he turns to Sister Clare and says: "You see? We were able to feed, clothe and educate our little world here – and help support an author too. And all of this just from a little vice! Kind of nice, isn't it?" They all laugh.

"We better leave before he wants to do it again" say the Peddlers. "Thanks, Clare. See you tomorrow!" They all exchange farewells as Sister Clare unlocks the door for them.

Dr. Frank remains with Sister Clare and continues the lesson after the Peddlers leave. "That's why you need money, Clare. It's the difference between being a kisser and a kissee."

"It's the difference between being a 'Francis Mendicant' and a 'Dr. Frank of the Franklin Bank'" adds Sister Clare, singing the jingle.

"I guess you could say that" responds Dr. Frank quite matter-of-factly.

"So tell me Doctor, why do you think *you* were able to grow so wealthy while Francis Mendicant seems to be so financially insecure?"

"Hard to say" he replies. "All I know is that I've worked hard my whole life. I had to spend *years* in medical school."

"Oh my, that really *is* a tragedy!" comments Sister Clare with a rare bit of sarcasm.

"Well, medical school is certainly not a place for panhandlers."

Sister Clare laughs a little as she washes one of the big pots that B.B. left with her. "Look, I'm a pan-handler too!"

But Dr. Frank remains serious. "I'm sure your friend is a good fellow. Maybe he just never applied himself enough."

"Oh, *that* must be the reason! He never applied himself enough. That *lazy* Francis Mendicant!" says Sister Clare in a scolding tone. "By the way, Doctor, do you happen to know what a Fundamental Attribution Error is?"

Dr. Frank wrinkles his forehead with exaggerated concentration. "A Fundamental Attribution Error? Hmmm. A Fundamental Attribution Error?" He then snaps his fingers and answers like a schoolchild: "Isn't that when somebody in a soup kitchen meets a wealthy person, and then with absolutely no knowledge of the situation, points to him and shouts 'GREEDY!' Is *that* what a Fundamental Attribution Error is?"

Sister Clare laughs a little, and then pointedly says "I happen to know that Francis Mendicant spent all of his savings to pay for his parents' medical bills."

After a short pause, Dr. Frank muses philosophically: "Well, that's just the way the machinery works, Clare. That's just the way the machinery works." After another pause he announces: "Well, Clare, I better get going now. Time is Money – or, in your case, Time is Poverty!" They both laugh. "Thanks for the conversation, Clare. Let's do it again someday."

"You know where to find me!" says Sister Clare as she walks him to the front door and unlocks it. They shake hands and wish each other well.

When the door closes, Sister Clare calls over to me: "Michael, I have some contraband cookies in my backpack. Can I share them with you? I need to clear my mind."

Pianos can get awfully dirty – and this old Lester has my hands caked with decades of dust. Normally I'd keep working and resist distractions. But the opportunity to be with Sister Clare and to eat contraband cookies at the same time? Yippee! I immediately drop my tools, jump up off the floor and run to wash my hands. Sister Clare seems to enjoy having company as she laughs and decompresses from her strange encounter with Dr. Frank of the Franklin Bank.

26. Doofus Gunshop Fountain-Flush

St. Louis is buried in snow this dreary February day. The drifts are so high they block the light from the hopper windows of our library meeting room. They also block the sound. It's hard to hear the outside traffic. Even the big church bells from across the street sound a bit muffled.

But muffled or not, those big bells can always be heard. And when they stop ringing Una forces a smile and announces "Welcome to the 16th meeting of the Machinists Union."

I don't expect that there will be any other smiles on display today. Earlier in the week there was a robbery at the Royal Brice Steakhouse. Mr and Mrs Bernardone, B.B.'s parents, were killed by a twenty-seven year-old drug addict.

B.B. is not here at our meeting today, of course, but Clare has come to help us get through this. She had been quite fond of B.B.'s parents and she tears-up whenever she speaks of them. Clare suggests that we not go to the Fountain Room this afternoon. We all agree.

As we talk about the police investigation, one of the newbies mentions: "I heard they traced the gun back to the Doofus Gunshop". This is no big surprise to any of us. Over the decades, many murder weapons have been traced back to the Doofus Gunshop.

"How come Doofus is still in business?" asks another newbie

"I wish they would just close that place down" says Coach. "It's a public nuisance."

"You wish?" gently asks our Professor.

That one comment leads to another and then to another, and before long we're planning for our next fountain-flush.

It takes some work to imagine how life might be different without guns. Those who go out to buy guns don't seem to have done this work. But those in jail have. Zero often tells us stories about people who imagine how different their lives would have turned out without guns. As a volunteer at Badluck Jail, he hears lots of them. He tells us that convicted gun users invariably regret having ever been introduced to guns. He hears the same from families who have suffered a gun accident or suicide in the home. They regret that a handgun was ever permitted in the house. Unfortunately, imagination is a lot easier in hindsight.

We want to stage our protest while the Royal Brice shooting is still fresh in the community's mind, so we decide to perform our fountain-flush this coming Saturday morning in front of the Doofus Gunshop.

We all pick jobs for ourselves. Everybody agrees to be an attractive Fountain - except for our Professor who again volunteers to be the Flush. A few of us volunteer to write a script. Several newbies volunteer to notify the neighbors about our plans. A couple other newbies volunteer to dress-up as police officers (after notifying the *real* St. Louis Police Department about the skit we have planned). I volunteer to write a song for us to chant, and Clare once again volunteers to provide television coverage. Come Saturday morning, we will be ready!

The Doofus Gunshop is a small, run-down clapboard building. Except for new bars in the windows, no work appears to have been done on the place for decades. The dilapidated white building with huge black letters spelling "Doofus Gunshop" painted on its sides blights the neighborhood today just as it blighted the neighborhood decades ago. Winter makes everything look even worse.

On Saturday morning we're all standing in the slush in front of the Doofus Gunshop, holding our picket signs. It's cold. As we sing, our breath condenses in the air as if we were smoking. But we're warmed to see so many neighbors come out to join us in the protest. As we chant: "NO MORE GUNS! NO MORE GUNS!" Sister Clare approaches with her camera technician from Channel 2 News. Clare holds one ear as she strains to talk into the microphone.

"Well, it's a noisy protest, that's for sure! If you can hear me over the chanting, I'll try to get comments from some of the participants." (*As Sister Clare turns to talk with one of our new young Fountain women, the singing and chanting stop.*) "Excuse me, may I ask why you've come to the rally today?"

The young woman answers: "My friends and I are here

for two reasons. The first reason, of course, is to shut down the Doofus Gunshop." (*We all cheer when she says this.*) She then continues: "And the second reason is to ask our fellow citizens – to *beg* our fellow citizens to collect any handguns they might have at home and destroy them – not to sell them, not to hide them, not to throw them away – *destroy* them."

Clare questions her: "Destroy them? How can a person destroy a handgun?"

The young woman dangles a little screwdriver from her keychain and says "With one of these. With a little screwdriver like this, a person can completely disassemble a gun – or 'disgunsemble' as we like to say."

All of us then enthusiastically chant "DISGUNSEMBLE! DISGUNSEMBLE!" until the young woman resumes speaking.

"Then all you have to do is throw away the little parts in different locations so they can never again be found and reassembled. So you see, it's quite easy to destroy a gun – even kind of pleasant! You should try it sometime!" (*We all chuckle supportively.*)

Clare thanks her and then turns to another new young woman: "And how about you? Do you think you'll be able to get *your* friends to destroy their handguns?"

She chuckles and replies: "*My* friends? None of us even *own* a handgun – never even *thought* about owning one. We were lucky to grow-up in families and in schools that taught us to love our neighbors as ourselves. Guns have no place in that kind of world." (*We all applaud supportively.*)

Clare thanks her and then turns to one of our new young Fountain men. "And you, sir? How do you feel about handguns?"

The young man calmly replies: "It's a fact that homes with guns are many times more likely to experience gun violence than homes without guns. It seems we could say the same thing about cities that have guns."

Clare asks: "Do you try to avoid gun-people like the others?"

"Avoid? No. I think that's a mistake" he replies. "You can't change people by avoiding them. Our goal is to *persuade* gun owners to destroy their own handguns. The only way we're going to be able to do that is by communicating with them – communicating why we feel that their guns will ultimately come to endanger our community."

Clare asks: "Do you really think they'll listen? Gun-people seem to have a bizarre need for their guns."

"I wouldn't say bizarre" answers the young man. "They just don't feel plugged-in to their community. They feel alone – feel fearful – feel that they won't be able to trust anybody when they need help. It's sad, but that's how they really feel. So having a gun is comforting to them. We're just lucky to be free from all of that. But we have to be sympathetic to those who aren't so lucky. Fear is a crippling emotion. It changes how people see the world."

Clare adds: "And I guess we shouldn't forget that they *do* have a legal right to own a handgun.

The young man quickly dismisses this line of reasoning: "People have a legal right to do *lots* of irresponsible things – things that would make life absolutely miserable if everybody were to do them."

Clare responds: "But gun owners seem to pride themselves on how *responsible* they are."

The young man again shakes his head in disagreement and says:

- "*Even the most responsible people* go through periods of **depression**.
- *Even the most responsible people* go through periods of **anger** and **mental instability**.
- *Even the most responsible people* can have their guns **stolen**.
- *Even the most responsible people* can have curious **children** who get into their things.
- *Even the most responsible people* can be **forgetful** – can make mistakes.
- And *even the most responsible people* will eventually **die**. What happens to the guns then?

So for all of these reasons and for countless more, being a gun-owner – even a so-called "responsible" one – ultimately puts the community in danger. And there's nothing responsible about that."

Clare asks: "So, what's the answer?"

"Communication" he replies. "Communication is *always* the answer. We need to allay their fears. We need to communicate to handgun owners that we're not against *them* – we're only against their weapons – weapons that we know will eventually come to hurt our community. We need to treat gun owners like the decent, responsible people that they want to be. But we also – in our most gentle voice – need to present the perspective of the community – the perspective that *all* handguns, no matter how responsible their owners are, will eventually cause us harm.

Clare asks: "Gentle persuasion? Don't you think that'll take a long time?"

"Well, sometimes nonviolence *takes* a long time. But it always gets the job done." (*We all cheer in concurrence.*) The young man continues: "So we need to keep talking, keep singing, and keep communicating until one by one we destroy each gun."

We all then begin chanting:

"ONE BY ONE, DESTROY EACH GUN!
ONE BY ONE, DESTROY EACH GUN!"

This is the cue for our Professor to approach from down the block. As he draws near wearing a tattered camouflage outfit and walking with a slightly inebriated gait, Clare stops him. "And you, sir? Why have *you* come to the rally?"

Our Professor removes the two cigarettes he has dangling from his mouth. He hacks and coughs. "What?" he snaps back with a grouchy voice. (*Meanwhile we're all still chanting.*)

Our Professor turns to us and shouts: "Shut up, you idiots!" None of us pay notice. He then turns to Clare and gruffly repeats "What?"

"Why have *you* come to the rally?"

"Rally? I ain't come to no rally. I come to Doofy's to gets me a lottery ticket. And if I gots any money left over, I'll gets me some cigarettes."

Clare asks him: "Are you 'for' or 'against' handguns?"

"Guns? I loves 'em. Guns is what makes us strong, baby! Guns is what makes us strong!"

Clare asks: "May I ask you some questions about guns?"

"Shoot away, baby!"

Clare slightly chuckles and then continues: "Well, that's just what I was going to ask you. Did you hear about the recent shooting at the Royal Brice Steakhouse?"

"Well, that's why we need more guns! To take care of them nutcases!"

Clare asks: "But like the previous gentleman explained, doesn't *everybody* have mental problems now and then?"

"Not me, baby!"

"Doesn't *everybody* have bouts of anger or fall into depression from time to time?"

"Not me, baby!"

"And what about burglars? What's to keep them from *stealing* the guns?"

"Burglars? Well that's why we need more guns, baby! That's why we need more guns! To take care of them nutcases!"

Clare, in a defeated voice, says "Okay". Then, after a short pause, she continues: "Would you at least support a gun tax to help pay for background checks and gun safety programs?"

Our Professor shouts back: "More taxes? No way, Jose! I ain't payin' no more taxes! No way, Jose! And don't tax my cigarettes either. Pick on somethin' else – like books – or broccoli." Our Professor then hacks and coughs into his hands. A yellow mucus coats his face and drips down from his beard as he continues his rampage: "Leave my cigarettes and my guns alone!"

Clare asks: "Do you support the 'Right to Carry' proposal?"

"Right to carry guns? I's already *got* that right, baby! I's already *got* that right. It's my *conchichooshinal* right! My *conchichooshinal* right!"

Clare asks: "But why in the world would you want to carry around a gun?"

"I just told you, it's my *conchichooshinal* right! My *conchichooshinal* right!

Clare wipes the spittle from her face, then continues: "But does your fascination with guns weigh more than the community's peace of mind? Many people in the community are *afraid* of guns."

"Afraid? Ha! Well them weenies *should* be afraid!" (He pulls a gun out from inside his jacket. Clare gasps.) "Them weenies *should* be afraid! Look at this little honey! Just look at 'er! Ain't she a cutie?"

Then several of us protestors notice the gun and shout

"Gun!" Our chanting stops.

Our Professor turns to us and taunts: "Ah you sissies, it ain't loaded!" (*He pulls the trigger and the gun discharges. There's some brief pandemonium and screaming in the crowd.*)

Our Professor shouts: "Them idiot neighborhood kids been playin' with it! Them idiot neighborhood kids!"

One of our newbies in her police uniform hurries over and grabs our Professor's hand. "Drop it" she commands.

Our Professor screams: "I ain't done nothin'! It was them idiot neighborhood kids!"

"Drop it!" she demands. The gun falls to the ground. She puts her foot on it. Then in a more gentle voice, she says: "Thank you. Please turn around and put your hands behind your back." As she puts handcuffs on our Professor, she dutifully informs him: "You have the right to remain silent."

Hearing this, we all erupt into cheers and resume our chanting: "NO MORE GUNS! NO MORE GUNS!"

Another newbie, also wearing a police uniform, arrives to help escort our Professor away. As he is being led away, our Professor can be heard crying out tantrum-like "Gimme back my gun! Gimme back my gun! Gimme back my gun!"

When he's in Flush mode, our Professor is not easy to forget. Unfortunately for us, several viewers watching at home remembered our Professor from the Testosterone Theater broadcast back in November. They complained to the Channel 2 director. Sister Clare was fired immediately for creating rather than reporting the news. It was quite a scandal - there was even an article about it in the Post-Dispatch. To make matters worse, we weren't successful in closing down the Doofus Gunshop. Doofus dug-in his heels and refused to move.

27. The Women Meet

✿

It's the third Sunday in March. Winter is finally losing its grip. One of the hopper windows in our library meeting room has been left slightly open - just enough for us to smell the sweet fragrance from the early hyacinths wafting in from the garden above, and just enough for the ringing church bells to come in loud and clear.

"Welcome to the 17th meeting of the Machinists Union" announces Una.

We've got a large group today - nearly thirty. I'm so happy to see that B.B. is with us again. I look at Sister Clare, then Una, and then back to B.B. They look so innocent. But I know they all have a secret - a big, big secret. Here's how I know:

Early one chilly evening at the beginning of the month, I stopped by the *B.B.Brice - Beans & Rice* restaurant after my classes to finish working on that old Lester spinet. I was on the floor replacing the crumbling elbows when Una and her roommate Daifu arrive.

"Hi Clare!" they shout as they come in through the fire exit.

"Hi you two! Perfect timing! I just finished cleaning-up."

"That *is* perfect timing!" laughs Daifu.

"Pick a table – I'll bring over some hot tea and crumpets to warm you up."

"Hot tea and crumpets? What are you doing with hot tea and crumpets inside a *B.B.Brice - Beans & Rice* restaurant? Isn't there some kind of law against that?" jokes Daifu.

"Oh, I keep all my contraband hidden" laughs Sister Clare. "*Beebs* doesn't even know about it! But Michael does!" When she points to me sitting on the floor behind the piano, they both warmly greet me – which makes me feel happy.

Sister Clare brings the treats over to her friends and sits down with them at their little table. "Where's Twimfina?" she asks.

"Zero came over to baby-sit."

"Zero?" chuckles Sister Clare.

"Don't laugh. They both like each other and when Zero starts rambling to her about this or that theory of child development, she's out like a light bulb!" They all laugh loudly.

"Here – this'll warm you up" says Sister Clare as she begins pouring the hot tea into their little cups. "Lemon balm and stevia."

"Mmm! Smells good!" says Daifu.

"How's B.B. coming along?" asks Una.

"Oh, his spirits are still down, but he's getting better" replies Sister Clare. After pouring the tea, she asks: "How about you, Daifu? How's medical school coming along this semester?"

"So far so good! I feel like I'm really getting into the thicket of things now" she replies.

"Do you know what kind of doctor she wants to be *this* week?" asks Una in a sarcastic tone while rolling her eyes.

"A rich one?" asks Sister Clare.

There's an uncomfortable silence. Then with a hurt voice, Daifu asks: "Why would you *say* such a thing, Clare?"

"Sorry – I guess I shouldn't have. I'm just afraid of losing you."

"*Losing* me?" asks Daifu.

"She's been lost for years" jokes Una.

"Yes, losing you" Sister Clare repeats. "I've been worrying about losing you ever since a doctor came into the restaurant a while back."

"Who?" asks Daifu.

"I'd rather not tell you his name since I don't have much good to say about him. But he came in and we somehow started talking about money. And he made it clear to me that his practice is to extract as much money from his patients as he possibly can – as if he were somehow *entitled* to it."

"And what does this have to do with me?" asks Daifu.

"Well, maybe this doctor didn't start-off that way. Maybe he started-off more like us. Maybe he was changed by some kind of *culture* that doctors slip into – some culture of entitlement. Maybe with drug companies and everybody else fawning over them – well, maybe that's just how doctors turn out these days whether they know it or not – or whether they *want* it or not."

After a long pause, Daifu responds: "Clare, in class we discussed a case study about a man who worked in a donut shop. He worked behind the counter – just like you do. In that environment he gained more than 200 pounds in less than two years. He got so heavy that he eventually lost his job and had to go on disability. A year later he was dead from heart failure."

Sister Clare interrupts her. "I know where this is going, Daifu – but it isn't the same – at least it doesn't *feel* the same. Your donut man didn't hurt anybody. Your donut man didn't violate the community's trust. Your donut man wasn't holding all of us by our genitals."

"Wow, Clare!" responds Una. "*You're* sure in a strange place tonight! What's going-on with you? Is it that Channel 2 job? Or B.B.? Or what?"

"No, Beebs and I are fine. And I couldn't care less about that so-called reporter's job. But you're right, I *am* in a strange place. I feel empty – like something's missing in my life. I'm not sure I can even put it into words. It's like I'm missing a feeling of community."

"Community? Well, don't you still volunteer with the Sisters of the Poor?" asks Una.

"No - and that's probably part of my problem. I'm so busy with school and with this place that I just don't have time to go there anymore. And it's not so much that I *physically* miss anything. It's just that I miss being part of their community. I *need* that in my life."

"How do you define community?" asks Daifu.

"I've been asking myself that very question" answers Sister Clare. "Who is my community? I think it's the people I want to **be** like".

"The people you want to **be** like?" repeats Una. "Well, I guess that cuts us out" she jokes.

"Of *course* I want to be like you and Daifu! But we're friends - best friends. That's not the same as a community."

"How about the Machinists Union?" asks Una.

"Yes, I really wish I could call them my community. But even though I love them - including you Michael! (she adds with a raised voice) - there's something missing from the recipe."

"You've got a recipe for community?" asks Daifu.

"Yes, I think I do. One ingredient seems to be a 'sense of mission'. When the Sisters work with the elderly, they're all working towards a common goal. This 'sense of mission' seems to bind them all together more than anything else."

"Well, we kind of have that with the Machinists Union, don't we?" asks Una.

"We do" answers Clare. "With our Ethics of Luck, I feel we really do have a strong sense of mission."

"Then we can scratch 'sense of mission' off the list" says Una. "Any other ingredients?"

"'Respect' seems to be an important one" continues Sister Clare. "I'm not sure where it comes from, but there always seems to be an atmosphere of respect among the Sisters. Even when they have their disagreements – and believe me, they have *plenty* of them – there's always this underlying love – this respect that keeps them together."

"Well, I guess we could always do better in *that* department" admits Una.

"I don't know if I'd say that" responds Sister Clare. "The Machinists always seem to be pretty decent to each other. I don't think we have much of a problem with 'respect.'"

"But there's still something's missing?" asks Una.

"Yes. And I think it has to do with 'time'. The Sisters spend lots of time together. They work together, they have their meals together, they pray together..."

"You think we should spend more time together?" asks Una.

"My friends, I think we should *live* together."

"*Live* together? Clare!" exclaim Una and Daifu as they both chuckle.

"Why not?" she pleads. "Why can't a group of *scientists* enjoy a communal life? Why can't a group of *scientists* share in a life of reflection and common purpose like our religious brothers and sisters do? Why can't a group of *scientists* pool together their time, their energy and their resources to achieve great things?"

"'Great things' aren't exactly on my agenda" jokes Una.

"Then *put* them there, Una!" says Sister Clare forcefully. "*Put* them there! Because I want to do this! And I can't do it without the two of you!"

"Do what?" they ask.

Sister Clare lowers her voice. "Look. This rat barn above us is going on the auction block sometime in the next couple of months."

"The hotel's being sold?" asks Daifu.

"Foreclosed" answers Sister Clare. "Please don't mention this to anybody because nobody knows about it yet. But Beebs has been talking with the bank. We think we can buy it."

"Buy the whole building?!" they both exclaim.

"It's a possibility. But I'm not going through with this unless you and the Machinists agree to move in here and live with us."

After a few seconds, Una says: "Clare, living with you and with the other Machinists would be a dream come true. But is this practical?"

"That's what I'm wondering too" adds Daifu. "How could we possibly get enough money to buy such a large building?"

"Well for starters, we'd have to sell the Royal Brice Steakhouse" answers Sister Clare.

"Sell the Royal Brice?!"

"And that's just to get the loan. We'll *still* need to pay the mortgage, we'll *still* need to gut the place and make it habitable, we'll *still* need to hire legal help to get though all the civil and criminal lawsuits hanging over the place like ripe fruit. For example, we just learned that the City is in the process of condemning the building because of all the fire and safety violations. Even the federal government is involved because of the drug crime."

"Wow – a perfect setting for some Victorian horror novel" chuckles Daifu.

"But we do have some strengths on our side" adds Sister Clare in a tone of confidence. "We have a healthy business, and we have a lease – a very good lease – a lease that's scaring away other buyers. I think B.B. must have foreseen this when he negotiated the contract."

"You know, it would really be *fun* living here" chuckles Una. "Twimfina would love it."

Daifu muses: "Who knows – maybe someday I could live here too and be the doctor for the Machinists Union."

Sister Clare jumps up and joyfully shouts: "Daifu, can I kiss you?"

"Sure. Unless you plan on charging me two dollars for it - which I didn't bring."

"Oh well then – forget it" says Sister Clare dismissively as she sits back down. They all laugh.

"So now you know why I called you here tonight. I needed to share this dream with you and ask for your help. I'm not worried about the 'financial' part. Beebs is doing the best he can to put that together. Either it'll happen or it won't. But I *am* worried about the 'community' part. I'm worried that the Machinists Union won't be able to survive here as a viable community. I'm worried that our Ethics of Luck won't be a strong-enough glue to keep us together."

"Well, it's kept us together for over a year now – and the group seems stronger than ever. I think our Ethics of Luck will *always* keep us together" says Una with confidence.

"Well then, let's make this our project" says Sister Clare. "You two deal with the 'community' part. Beebs and I will deal with the financial nuts and bolts. Agreed?"

"Agreed!"

"Did you hear this, Michael?" shouts Sister Clare to me. You're our secretary – we really need you. Will you help us?"

"Yes" I answer in one word. (I never think of clever things to say until the following day. But my mind is in a whirl of excitement. I can sense that something big is happening.)

28. Flophouse Dreams

April. We're not meeting in the library today. Instead we're meeting here in the new *B.B.Brice - Beans & Rice* restaurant. Una had asked me to notify everybody about our change of venue. I called everybody yesterday, and to be safe I dropped by the library this morning and taped a note to the meeting room door.

I doubt that any of the newbies have ever been here before. At least I *hope* they've never been here, given the reputation of the upstairs hotel.

At one time the Franklin Majestic Hotel had been quite a respectable place – in fact President Franklin D. Roosevelt (who was then governor of New York) spent two nights here during the 1932 presidential campaign. At that time there was gold carpeting in all the halls and small chandeliers hung in the hallways – one above each guest's door. The Franklin Majestic also had a sumptuous lobby that opened into a celebrated restaurant.

A few decades later the word "Majestic" was dropped from its name. By then it had become unlikely that any presidential candidate would ever want to stay at the Franklin Hotel. The gold carpeting no longer sparkled. Many of the small chandeliers above the doors had become dark. The once-celebrated restaurant had withered into an obscure lounge. About the only reminder of its 'Majestic' past was a large photographic print of President Roosevelt that hung on the lobby wall at the exact location where he had once stood, puffing on that long cigarette holder.

More decades passed. Today even the word "Hotel" is sometimes dropped from its name. All of St. Louis – especially the police – now refer to the place as the "Franklin Flophouse". Many things are different now. For example, the large presidential print in the lobby is gone – stolen years ago. Around the same time the Health Department closed the lounge during a rat infestation.

Although many things are different, some things remain exactly the same. For example, the carpeting in the halls is still the same. Of course it's soiled beyond recognition and many of its rips have been mended with tape – but it's still the same carpeting. And the metal brackets from the little chandeliers still hang above each guest's door. Of course their dangling little crystals have long since disappeared. But the brackets still hang there like some kind of twisted spider. And there's something else in the Franklin Flophouse that just might be the same: the air. The entire place reeks of tobacco and urine. Who knows, even President Roosevelt's cigarette smoke might still linger up there.

But down here in the *B.B.Brice - Beans & Rice* restaurant it is clean and bright. Everything is painted white, save for the two red fire extinguishers hanging on opposite walls. The group seems impressed as they arrive for our meeting.

"Sorry we don't have enough chairs for everybody" announces Sister Clare. "Please feel free to sit on the floor. I just cleaned it recently."

"How recent is recent? asks Coach.

"February" she answers. Everybody laughs.

Twimfina is sitting on the piano bench - cautiously plunking this key and that key - fascinated with the music machine.

Una is standing in front of the counter. She checks her wristwatch. It's time to start. She calls over to Twimfina who slides off the piano bench and hurries over to stand next to her mother.

"Welcome to the 18th meeting of the Machinists Union" Una announces. She pauses and looks around. There are about thirty of us again. We're all in a big circle. She and Twimfina are standing at its head. Several seniors, a pregnant woman, and our Professor are seated in white plastic chairs. The rest of us are sitting cross-legged on the floor.

"So much has happened to us recently" begins Una. "Some of it horrible..." (she looks at B.B. and bows her head slightly) "... and some of it wonderful." (She again looks at B.B. and smiles.) "Today we're focusing on the wonderful."

"Get used to this place because we'll probably be meeting here from now on. B.B. has sold the Royal Brice." (There's an exhale of astonishment from those who haven't yet heard the news.) "And he's bought this building" (Another wave of astonishment whirls around the circle.)

"The Franklin Flophouse?" shouts a newbie.

"Yes, but now we'll probably want to come up with a better name for it" chuckles Una "because B.B. and Clare have invited all of us to live here with them." (It suddenly becomes breathlessly quiet.) "They want us to live with them as a Community - a Community of Machinists."

It's totally silent as the words try to sink in.

"Would we be naked?" asks a pudgy, middle-aged man.

"No - but we'll make an exception for you" answers Una. Everybody laughs.

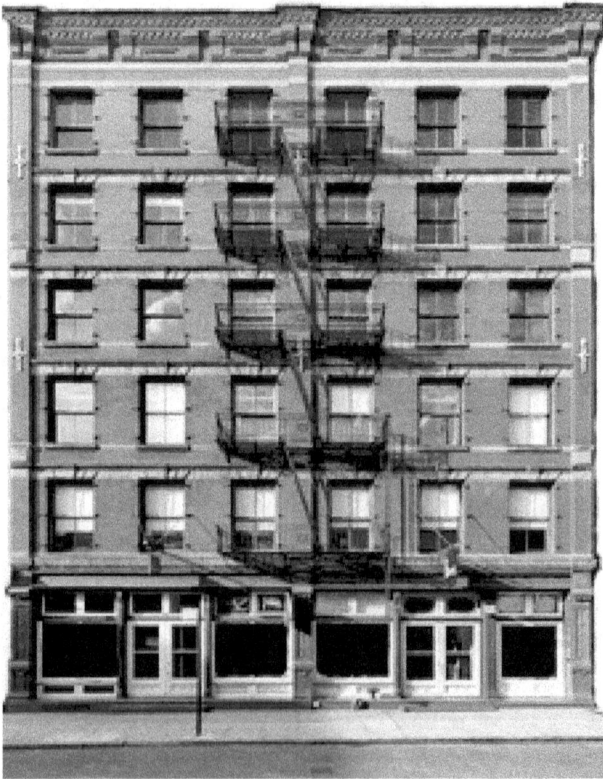

Franklin Flophouse

Then one of the newbies asks: "How would it work? How would we pay our bills?"

Una answers: "Well, we'd have to keep operating the kitchen and restaurant as we do now. Hopefully we can expand and add more carts. In addition, this coming semester we plan to start a high school on the bottom two floors of the building." (There's a stir of surprise from everybody.) "The high school will probably be a financial drain for a while, but eventually it'll pull its own weight."

Somebody else asks "Since B.B. owns the restaurant and the building, will we all be working for him?"

"No. We'll all be working for the Community. I haven't explained it yet, but B.B. has offered to turn over the building and the 'Beans & Rice' business to the Community if we can sustain ourselves."

We all look over at B.B., dumbfounded that he's willing to give away everything he owns. "What in the world has Sister Clare done to your brain?" we secretly wonder.

B.B. isn't exactly smiling. He has an inscrutable expression of mixed emotion on his face - a constipated sort of grin - a distraught half-smile. It reminds me of faces I've seen at funeral homes when bereaved ones are approached by total strangers who want to express their condolences.

"Does anybody really think we can just snap our fingers and start a high school?" asks another newbie with incredulity in her voice.

Una snaps her fingers and points to Coach, who seems eager to answer.

"Nobody mentioned anything about snapping fingers" Coach begins. "We know it'll be difficult, but there's no reason we can't do it. Look at all the great high schools we already have in St. Louis. There's Visitation, St. Joseph's, Ursuline, Cor Jesu, De Smet, Chaminade... and probably a dozen more. If religious people can do it using their faith as the foundation, why can't we science people do the same thing using our Ethics of Luck as the foundation?"

"Would we be the teachers?" asks the same newbie.

"We'd have to be. We couldn't swing it otherwise. Of

course we'd have to study teaching and eventually get our credentials. But we already have lots of expertise, especially in the sciences. Some of us, like Una, Sister Clare, Zero, Michael and I will be graduating with science degrees in just a few weeks. In addition our own talent, we've also got experienced teachers like our Professor and my father to help guide us."

"I'm sorry to bring up the subject of money again" begins another newbie "but I just don't understand how we'll get paid."

"We won't" replies Una with only two words. (Everybody chuckles.) "This is a commune. We work for the common good. Just pretend it's a monastery and we've all taken a vow of poverty."

Zero interjects: "By the way, there's no need to ever apologize for asking questions about money. We *all* need to ask questions about money. I have a personal story about this that I'll never forget. Two summers ago I joined a commune down in the Ozarks. It was a beautiful place in the middle of Mark Twain National Forest. There were a couple dozen of us. We pooled our money together into an expense account to pay for necessities. Three weeks later the whole commune fell apart because of bickering about what was or wasn't a necessity. So that's why money needs to be discussed beforehand and why things need to be spelled out on paper. I also remember my grandparents telling me about a kibbutz they used to live on in Israel. They and several other kibbutzniks came to feel that the wealth wasn't being shared equitably. This caused a lot of bitterness."

"Maybe we could all be candelescent" I suggest.

"Candelescent?" asks Una. "What's *that*?"

"Candelescent - like a candle" I reply. "We burn brightly during our lives and then when it's all over there's nothing left but a world made better by the light and the warmth we've given off." (*This is an idea that popped into my mind last year when we were standing on the church steps holding candles during a Peace Vigil.*) There's a long, long silence in the group. I feel a little embarrassed, but at least I don't hear anybody laughing. Then a newbie says "Uh-huh" slowly and sarcastically. Everybody laughs.

Sister Clare finally asks the crucial question: "Could I please see a show of hands of those who might consider living here with us?" A large number of us raise our hands - certainly more than half. Sister Clare smiles, visibly relieved.

"When is all of this going to start?" asks a newbie.

Sister Clare answers: "Not until the building is clean and safe. We want our home to be a healthy place. That means we've got to tear out all the old carpeting, fix all the leaking radiators, rewire all the rooms, paint all the walls, sand and varnish all the floors. It'll probably take us all summer to get it done."

"Just so we get it finished by Labor Day so we can start the new high school on time" adds Coach.

"How long is this Community thing supposed to last?" asks a newbie.

"To the very end – *Usque ad Finem*" answers Zero, slowly and loudly, enunciating the Latin words as if he were a Roman orator. Una and Twimfina look at each other, smile and roll their eyes.

Our meeting continued for quite a while. We discussed all kinds of things, from what kind of food we should stock to what equipment we should outfit the classrooms with.

Eventually B.B. and Sister Clare bring out the bowls for this month's taste test. 'Lemon-Limas' is the name of the dish - a real favorite of mine.

While we're comparing the flavors of the three bowls, we begin tossing around names for our new high school. The first ones weren't serious - sardonic names about torturing students or facetious ones named after disreputable scientists. But in time we narrowed it down to two names: 'Mendel Science High' and 'Machinists Union High'. I personally preferred the later and probably would have prevailed had there not been so many newbies voting. Long before the newbies appeared on the scene, we had agreed to neither idolize nor demonize people. Although I have always admired the Father of Genetics, naming a school after somebody is pretty high idolatry as I see it. But we oldies apparently haven't passed this reasoning along to the newbies - and now we're paying for it.

As a result of our voting, the official name of our school is now "Mendel Science High". Oh well. At least we're not named after some politician, like lots of schools are. Some of the newbies are already referring to the upstairs living quarters as "Mendel

Monastery". I guess it's not the worst of names considering the fact that Gregor Mendel himself was a monk when he was growing his pea plants in the monastery's garden - and changing the world. Mendel Monastery. The alliteration's kind of nice too.

29. Badluck Jail Fountain-Flush

✦

May. Today is a gloriously beautiful day in St. Louis. The adage 'April showers bring May flowers' has once again proven itself true. There are flowers everywhere. Even here in this rundown commercial area there are countless dandelions pushing up along the curb and in the cracks of the broken sidewalk.

Yesterday UMSL had their graduation ceremony and at least a half dozen of us received diplomas. Several people are congratulating Zero for some special honor he had won. But before I can say anything to Zero, Coach asks me:

"Michael, I didn't see you yesterday."

"I know. Technically I haven't graduated." I reply.

"Why not?" he presses with some alarm in his voice.

"I just never applied for graduation."

"Why? Did you miss the deadline?"

"No, Coach. I just wasn't interested. That piece of paper isn't important to me."

"That, my friend, is a mistake. Listen, you need to submit that paperwork! We need you to help teach in Mendel Science High! If money's the problem, I'll be happy to pay for it! I know that impulse to turn away from the trappings of academia. I feel it myself. But this is the one time you've got to resist it."

"Thank you, Coach. But it's no impulse. I know what I'm doing."

Meanwhile Una is looking at her wristwatch and announces: "Welcome to the 19th meeting of the Machinists Union."

Coach exhales loudly, then softly says to me: "We'll continue this conversation later" as he heads back to his place in the circle. Zero, who is sitting on the floor next to me, puts his hand on my shoulder and whispers "Good job!"

Maybe the real reason I didn't apply for graduation is that my father never went to college, save for a night class or two. Years ago I overheard him telling my mother about a meeting he attended. All the other men sitting around the table were wearing college rings. My father said he covered his hand so that nobody could see his bare fingers. I can't get that image out of my mind. And this is no ordinary man covering his hand. Except when it comes to politics, this is the most rational, clearest-thinking, education-loving person that I know. And the reason he never went to college is because he was always working to pay for my own education. Believe me, I have absolutely no interest in ever, *ever* wearing one of those rings.

We begin the meeting with a discussion of the work we're doing on the building upstairs - our Mendel Science High and the residence rooms. Although we hired professionals for some of the jobs (fixing the leaky steam radiators, replacing the leaking and stuck flushometer valves on the toilets, rewiring the electric), we're doing most of the other work ourselves. Our big accomplishment since last time is that we removed all the drapes and the carpeting. We did it by connecting a chute from each fire escape to a dumpster down in the street. With all the carpet padding and the dirt, we undoubtedly removed *tons* of stuff! We also got rid of all the hideous ornamentation - like those chandelier frames that used to hang above each door.

During a lull in our discussion, B.B. and Sister Clare bring out the 'A-B-C' bowls for another taste-test. This time the dish is called 'Potato-Tomato Lentils'. Every month I seem to discover a new favorite!

It's Zero's turn again to give the Presentation. His topic is the famous 'Stanford Prison Experiment'. As he speaks he passes around actual photographs of the experiment. Although Una often gets exasperated when Zero goes off on tangents, he's actually a very good storyteller. He has us all captivated - at least until the very end when the narrative stops and he tries to explain the significance of the experiment in language that is much too technical.

One of the newbies - a grandmotherly sort of older woman - politely interrupts to offer her own summary: "The moral of the story is that 'when good people are put into an evil place, bad things happen."

Those words 'good, bad, and evil' are hard for us Machinists to deal with. We usually don't describe people as 'good' or 'bad'. And we certainly would never use the word 'evil'. It's pretty clear that there are going to be some growing pains, some tensions as we oldies try to change the newbies - or the newbies change us. It's possible that these new folks aren't even determinists!

But Zero graciously and warmly responds with: "Thank you! That's a *much* better way of putting it! 'When good people are put into an evil place, bad things happen.' That's beautiful!"

The same newbie continues: "And if bad things happen when good people are put into evil places, then we should work to make sure our prisons are not evil places."

Zero's patience has paid off. He smiles as the rest of us voice our agreement. Yes, we should work to make sure our prisons are not evil places. Although it's got that un-Machinist word 'evil' in it, this is exactly what Zero has forever been preaching.

Then a young, energetic newbie suggests: "Let's walk down to Badluck Jail and rally in support of the 'Model Prison Bill'. They'll be voting on it in Jeff City this week."

So here we are, three hours later, marching on the steps of Badluck Jail in downtown St. Louis. We're here with freshly-made signs to demonstrate our support of the Model Prison Bill. Trying our best to be attractive Fountains, we're all cleanly dressed and smiling. We all hold respectful protest signs as we march 'round and 'round in a big loop, chanting:

> *"Pass the Model Prison Bill*
> *Educate with Useful Skills*
> *Pass the Model Prison Bill*
> *Educate with Useful Skills"*

I feel kind of happy that we're here doing this. Advocating for better prisons seems like an appropriate mission for us Machinists. As determinists we understand that prisoners have been dealt a bad hand in life – a hand that's missing some cards. We want prisons to be places where these missing cards can be replaced. It's not an impossible job - teachers do it every day.

After only ten minutes or so of marching and chanting, we are surprised to see television crews from both Channel 4 and Channel 5 arriving. How did they find out about this?

"Clare, your competition's here!" jokes Coach.

Actually, this is good news to us. It's important that we be seen and found attractive by as many people as possible – and television's the best way to get this done.

Because of Badluck's uneven steps, we have to watch where we're walking. But as we glance up now and then, we notice someone in the distance approaching with a sign. The person doesn't seem to be walking very steadily, stumbling a bit to this side and that side as if inebriated. We can now make out a gray beard and realize it's an old man.

Coach is the first to recognize him and choke out his name: "Professor?" A number of us stumble on the steps and have to regain our footing.

Sure enough, it's our Professor. And like always, he's a tragic sight. He's wearing a long black winter overcoat that's dragging on the pavement. His beard is all greasy. And did I mention the pink shower cap? Like always, it's devastating to see the old man reduced to this. But like always it's surreally comical at the same time. I can't look at him, yet I can't *not* look at him either. We keep chanting and try to ignore him. But when our Professor's in 'Flush mode', he's un-ignorable.

Although he's much closer now, we still can't read his sign. The wind keeps buffeting it in all directions – plus the sloppy lettering looks like it was written with shoe polish. Worse yet, he's holding the thing upside-down!

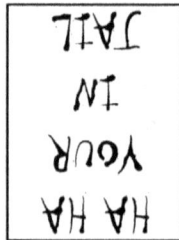

```
┌─────────────┐
│     JAIL    │
│             │
│      IN     │
│             │
│     YOUR    │
│             │
│    HA HA    │
└─────────────┘
```
(shown upside-down)

Although *we* can't make-out the sign yet, we know the news teams can because they suddenly light-up as if they've all just won the lottery. As the cameras turn towards our Professor and the reporters rush over to him, waving their microphones, the old man raises his sign high to share his wisdom with the world:

'HA-HA YOUR IN JAIL'

The sign makes no sense, plus he's using the possessive pronoun "your" instead of the contraction, plus nobody beyond the fourth grade would ever express anything so idiotic.

None of the reporters seem to recognize him from earlier fountain-flushes. Apparently the Channel 4 and Channel 5 news teams don't watch the Channel 2 News. The questions start immediately. Although the reporters use kind words and superficially treat him like a respectable citizen with a legitimate opinion to share, you can be sure they're absolutely thrilled to have a genuine lunatic in their net.

"Excuse me, sir. Have you come to rally for prison reform?"

"Has I come to rally for *prison* reform? You *bet* I has, sonny! You *bet* I has! Reform it back into a prison! That's what I say – reform it back into a prison! A *real* prison – not some fancy country club!"

"What kind of reforms do you have in mind?"

"Throw out all them television sets! Throw out all them air conditioners! Throw out all them pillows! Throw out all them prison-burgers!"

"Prison-burgers?"

"That's right. I hear them prison-burgers is real thick. I hear them prison-burgers is real juishee. I hear them prison-burgers… (*saliva drools from our Professor's mouth, sticking to his beard as he tries to wipe it away*) ah look! now you gots me shlobberin' all over the place!"

"It seems like you want the prison to be more punitive."

"I wants the prison to be more like a *prison*! The judge didn't say 'Look you scumbag, I'm sending you on a vacation!' No, he said 'Look you scumbag, I'm sending you to *prison*! And that's what I want. Prison! Real prison! Make 'em suffer! Make 'em squirm! Learn 'em all a lesson! That's what I say – learn 'em all a lesson!"

"But doesn't violence always lead to more violence?"

"Then knock it out of 'em! Knock it out of 'em 'til they

behaves! Bang them heads together! That's how they learned *me*! Bang them heads together!"

"But isn't there a difference between telling prisoners they've made a mistake and telling them they're worthless?"

"Well they *is* worthless! They *is* worthless!"

"But someday these people are going to be released. Wouldn't you prefer that they come out of prison with good working skills?

"I prefers that they *never* comes out!"

"How do you feel about the death penalty?"

"How I feels about the death penalty? "Whoopee!" *That's* how I feels about the death penalty! "Whoopee!" You murder, then you *gets* murdered! Make it even – that's what I say! Make it even! Even Steven! Same for them perverts! Same for them terrorists! You can throw in a few Yankee fans too for all I care!"

(*By now the reporters are no longer able to stifle their laughter. The journalistic pretense is gone. It's now pure entertainment.*)

"Would you ever consider life in jail without parole?"

"Life in jail? (*reflectively*) Ya mean sittin' 'round all day watchin' TV and eatin' prison-burgers? (*pause*) Yeah sonny! – *I'd* consider it! Sign me up!"

(*The reporters laugh heartily. Our Professor has once again become an object of ridicule.*)

"You seem to believe in the old Hammurabi 'Eye for an eye – Tooth for a tooth' way of doing things."

(*Our Professor sticks his fingers in his mouth and pulls out his dentures and 'gums' his answer:*) "I ain't *got* no teesh!"

30. Everyday Machinists

⚙

June. This is supposed to be our 20th meeting, but it feels different - even disorganized. We're downstairs together in the *B.B.Brice - Beans & Rice* restaurant. B.B. hasn't come down yet. I still hear the whirring of a floor sander upstairs. A lot of us are sitting on the floor, but there are too many of us to make a circle. It looks more like an amoeba. Una is sitting at the head of the amoeba next to her daughter. According to my watch, she should have formally opened the meeting several minutes ago. I guess she doesn't want to interrupt the discussion that is going on.

Sister Clare says "Wow, there must be forty of us today! B.B.'s going to be so surprised when he comes down! Every time we do a fountain-flush we get lots of new members!"

"I've been thinking about those fountain-flushes" responds a newbie. "Do they really work? I mean look at the results: Doofus is still open for business, and that 'Enemia' film just came out on DVD."

Our Professor jokes: "It did? Finally! I'll have to run out and get me one of those!" (*Everybody laughs.*)

Zero reflects: "I have to say, Professor, that of all the activities we've done, my favorite is still our fountain-flush at the Testosterone."

"Mine too!" jokes our Professor. "I just *loved* them fishies!" (*Everybody laughs again.*)

A curious newbie asks our Professor: "Were those really fish in your mayonnaise?"

"Oh, you wanna know my secrets, huh?" replies our Professor. (*We all chuckle.*)

"Well, first of all, it wasn't mayonnaise. That would have killed me on the spot. Even the *thought* of mayonnaise makes me gag. I ain't no martyr. That jar was full of sweet vanilla yoghurt. I bought a few tubs of it that morning. And my right hand was very clean when I went digging for them fishies, which, by the way, were just pieces of that wiggly candy. No, I ain't no martyr." (*We chuckle and even applaud a little.*)

But the newbie wants to know even more: "Did you really buy a ticket and watch that movie when you got inside?"

"I did indeed buy a matinee ticket – not too bad with the senior discount. But I've never had much interest in watching that movie. So I just went into the restroom and washed-up and changed my clothes. The place was pretty empty, so I was able to take my time. After I got cleaned-up, I sat down next to the pop-corn machine and read my book and ate my yoghurt and listened to all the commotion you all were making outside. It was the best ticket I ever bought! I had a *good* ol' time – a *good* ol' time!" (*He speaks these words just as he had spoken them into Sister Clare's microphone. We all laugh and fully applaud.*)

(Although the newbie didn't ask him, here are a couple more of our Professor's secrets - these from the Doofus Gunshop protest. That yellow mucus he coughed-up onto his beard when he was smoking two cigarettes at the same time was just lemon pie filling. Like me, our Professor loves lemon meringue pie. He had a packet of the pie filling in his hand and smashed it against his face as he hacked and coughed. Another little secret is that the gun our Professor used was just a starter pistol used to start races. Coach had lent it to him. It sure looked real on TV!)

Our Professor continues: "We've been getting some public recognition lately. I guess there might be something good in that. But what do our *families* say? What do *they* say about our Machinists Union? Do your parents or your children or your spouse feel that our Ethics of Luck has brought something good to their lives? How about the people at work? It's one thing to play the role - the heroic role - of an active pacifist when we're dancing in front of the television cameras. But how well do we dance when we're at home or at work where all those annoying people are? (*We chuckle a little.*) How heroic are we *then*? How pacifistic are we *then*? We spend most of our time discussing how to implement our 'Ethics of Luck' on a *grand* stage. But the Oscar should probably go to those who can make the 'Ethics of Luck' live and breathe on their own *little* stages. That's the challenge – not so much to be the 'Laurence Olivier Machinist', but to be an 'Everyday Machinist'. So that's my question. How can we best be Everyday Machinists?"

Coach is the first to respond: "The best way to be an Everyday Machinist is to get off any 'teams' we're on."

"Any *teams* we're on?" we echo.

"Yes, we've got to get off any teams we're on. It's a lesson straight from the Genocide Slide. The Slide *warns* us about grouping ourselves into a 'team'. It *warns* us against having any 'Hooray for our Side' feelings." (*Coach then sings a verse from the familiar sports cheer:*)

"Hooray for our side! Hooray for our side!
Got the glory, got the pride – Hooray for our side!"

"What an ugly song" he continues. "As a coach I have to listen to that obscene thing constantly. If people wouldn't get so emotionally wrapped-up with a team, they'd be able to stay connected to those who don't *belong* to the team."

"A coach who's against teams?" asks our Professor.

"I'm not against participating on *sports* teams – I'm not against competition – in fact I think competition can be something good. After all, to form a competition, people have to cooperate and work together. No, I'm talking about a different *kind* of team – a team that thrives on a *lack* of cooperation – a self-admiring, self-aggrandizing, self-righteous tribal sort of team – (*he pauses*) – I'm not even sure I can find the right words."

Sister Clare tries to help him: "A team that people don't just *belong* to, but one that they actually *become*."

"Exactly" continues Coach. "They *become* the team – they share the same bloodstream with the team – they see the team as an extension of themselves – something they feel a need to defend from outsiders. I mean it's one thing to *favor* a Democratic idea or to *favor* a Republican idea, but it's quite another thing to *be* a Democrat or to *be* a Republican, or to *be* a Christian, or to *be* a Jew, or to *be* a Socialist, or to *be* a Capitalist, or to *be anything*!"

Our Professor asks "To be a Machinist?"

"Right! Even to be a Machinist! Maybe we shouldn't call ourselves 'Machinists'. What *good* does it do? It's just one more wall, one more division, one more label that separates us from the rest of the world."

"Thank you, Coach – well-spoken!" responds our Professor. We all applaud Coach. I've never heard him speak so passionately.

Our Professor then asks: "Can anybody think of another way we can be 'Everyday Machinists'?" He waits a few seconds. "Do we happen to know somebody in a desperate situation whom we could help by being Everyday Machinists? ...Someone facing an empty future? ...Someone for whom we need to look below the surface at the actual spinning gears and wheels to understand why he did the horrible thing that he did?

A chill sweeps through our group as we realize he's talking about Dougie-the-druggie, the young man who shot B.B.'s parents.

"If we're going to be Everyday Machinists" our Professor continues, "then we have to be Machinists every day – not just on the third Sunday of the month. If we're going to be Everyday Machinists, then we have to look for and see the machinery in *everybody* – not just in the people we love. I imagine there are machine shops all over the world that eventually have to deal with a machine they've never seen before. I imagine there are machine shops all over the world that sooner or later will have to face their ultimate test. Dougie just might be ours. Let's do it right."

Hooray for Our Side!

Secretary Michael

Hoo-ray for our side! Hoo-ray for our side! Got the glo-ry, got the pride,

Hoo-ray for our side! We're the good and right-eous ones!

Wave the flag and shoot the guns for our side, that's who [hoo - hoo - hoo]*
*[monkey-like]

31. Lauterkeit

⚙

"Welcome to the 21st meeting of the Machinists Union" says Una with a smile.

It's July. About forty of us are down here in the *B.B.Brice - Beans & Rice* restaurant. We're all enjoying these new chairs that we'll eventually have to move upstairs when Mendel Science High gets started in a few weeks. Upstairs from the school is our future home, Mendel Monastery. Nobody feels very sure about any of this. So far only eleven of us have made a commitment to live here.

Although B.B. has already moved in, the building is legally still considered condemned and unfit for occupancy. But it won't be condemned for long. Lots of progress has been made over the past couple of months. The wiring is finished. All the toilets work. The cast iron radiators no longer leak. The elevator is safe. The walls have been repaired and primed. The maple floors have been sanded. All the vermin are gone.

Meanwhile, Coach has assumed responsibility for Mendel Science High. He's been recruiting new students all summer. So far about sixty have signed-up. He and his father have also been working with us prospective teachers, helping us to prepare thoughtful and effective lesson plans.

For many of us, joining this Community is the gamble of our lives. Una will have to quit her coveted job at the Missouri Botanical Garden. I'll have to give notice at Academy Piano Service. Zero will have to give up his apartment. Coach will have to give up his baseball and soccer league jobs. I've never been much of a gambler, so I worry about what may lay ahead.

"Secretary Michael, where did we leave off?" asks Una.

Glancing at my notebook I answer "We were talking about ways we could be Everyday Machinists - ways we could apply our Ethics of Luck at home."

"Does anybody have any comments on this before we move on?" asks Una. (A newbie in a wheelchair raises his hand.)

"Yes? Lauterkeit?"

"My comment is that we should have more than just fountain-flushes in our toolbox. There are lots of situations where fountain-flushes just won't work. We need other tools."

"Like what?"

"Like an Incompat."

"A nincompoop?" jokes Coach. Everybody laughs.

"No, an Incompat" repeats Lauterkeit. An Incompat is some narrative we create which is *incompatible* with the narrative we want to extinguish. I'll use myself as an example. Suppose there's a narrative that those of us with mobility problems are lazy and just sit around all day watching TV. We could weaken that ugly stereotype by creating an Incompat - a story or film that shows someone like me in a wheelchair working hard at several jobs. A person can't be working several jobs and still be lazy at the same time. The stories are incompatible with each other! Something's got to give."

Zimbo is the first to gives his imprimatur. "The psychology of it makes perfect sense!" he says.

"Does an Incompat have to be a film?" asks Coach.

"No. It could be a drawing, a song, a rumor, anything - anything that sets up an incompatibility." replies Lauterkeit.

"This would be a great tool for artists" comments a newbie.

"We artists change the world!" chuckles Una, who just graduated with a degree in Art (in addition to her Plant Science degree)."

We spend quite a while talking about Incompats and how we might best use them. We agree that this tool would be especially useful for Mendel Monastery because we'd be living together and could more easily schedule rehearsals.

This month's Presentation is given by a newbie. Ginny Jean (one of the Jean twins) has a background in infectious diseases. The title of her talk is 'Brains Controlled by Bugs'.

Ginny explains how some parasites and infectious microbes have evolved an ability to change the behavior of their current hosts so they can more easily spread to new hosts. She gives many wonderful examples. She tells us about:

- pathogens that spread by causing their human hosts to cough and sneeze;
- the rabies virus that spreads by causing infected animals to

salivate and bite other animals;

- the toxoplasma parasite that spreads by causing infected rodents to lose their fear of cats (in whose digestive system the parasite deposits eggs);
- parasitic hairworms (which reproduce in water) that spread by causing infected grasshoppers to jump into water and drown themselves;
- the malaria parasite Plasmodium that spreads by causing infected mosquitoes to visit more hosts;

After the Presentation, Ginny invites us to ask questions. Lauterkeit raises his hand. "Yes?"

"The whole idea of this bothers me – it's like we don't have a free will. I've been thinking about this a lot recently. It's really a sickening, empty feeling that I just can't get out of my head."

Well, this comment sounds way too familiar to those of us who were in EP101. In fact if we were working for the fire department, we'd be sliding down the pole right now because this is as close to an alarm bell as we'll ever hear. So before Ginny is able to respond, our Professor stands and addresses Lauterkeit himself:

"You're not alone, Lauterkeit, you're not alone. I imagine most of us here have come to that same conclusion. And you're right – it does make a person feel kind of sick and empty. Many of us have suffered those same feelings."

"But the sickness doesn't last forever, Lauterkeit" adds Una. "And you've got all of us to help you with the emptiness."

"Yes, you've got all of us to help you with the emptiness" repeats our Professor.

"And later you'll even find that something good comes from all this pain and confusion" predicts Zero. "It teaches compassion. You'll see people differently."

"Yes, it'll change your life" promises our Professor.

Hearing Una, Zero and our Professor coax Lauterkeit off the ledge and into the safety of the Machinists Union is very moving to me. I feel like I'm in the company of professionals. And not only is this exchange helpful to Lauterkeit, it's also good for our whole group. It puts us all on the same page. If we didn't know it before, all forty of us know it now that the Machinists Union is an organization of determinists – determinists who have found an ethical dimension to their understanding. This ethical dimension - this 'Ethics of Luck' as we call it - is the very glue that holds us together.

32. Things Could Have Been Different

☼

August. It hasn't rained all month, but this has been good for us. It has given us the chance to leave open all the windows on the bottom three floors of the building to vent away the paint fumes. So far, we've only finished the bottom three stories, but they're the only ones we absolutely need. The 1st and 2nd floors will be used for the school. The 3rd floor will serve as our living quarters until the upper floors are completed.

The old hotel looks totally different inside. The walls used to be dark and ornately decorated. Now they've all been painted a simple white. There used to be soiled gold carpeting throughout. Now the sanded maple flooring is bare, protected by several layers of clear varnish which gives it the natural glow of a gymnasium floor. The halls are so smooth and clean we slide around on them in our socks.

With the bottom three stories habitable, the twelve of us who have made a commitment to live here have begun moving in. B.B.'s been living on various floors for a couple of months already, sleeping on a cot wherever he happens to be working. But now he's picked one of the twenty rooms on the 3rd floor along with the rest of us. Besides B.B. and me, our Community includes Sister Clare, Zero, Coach, Una (with her daughter Twimfina), Grandma E (a name she chose), Lauterkeit, Daifu, Simi, and the Jean twins (Ginny and Julie). There are eight rooms left over, so we've designated one of them as our 'Community Room'. The twelve of us have agreed to meet there every night before we go to bed for an 'Evening Meeting'.

As for the school, Coach has his teaching staff in place and feels confident that they'll start on schedule September 3rd, the day after Labor Day, exactly 16 days from today. It's been a huge juggling act for him to accommodate everybody's different schedules. For example, some of the teachers will be attending graduate school. And all of us - Coach included - have daily duties with the Beans & Rice business and with maintaining the building. So many schedules!

Since most of us teachers have science backgrounds, the new school will be able to provide a very rich science program (which is undoubtedly the main reason we've been able to attract so many students to this odd downtown location).

But Science is not the only subject in life. (Actually, I could argue that Science is *indeed* the only subject in life, but I won't.) Fortunately we're diverse enough to cover all the required subjects. For example, Lauterkeit (a law student at St. Louis University) will teach History. Grandma E (an older woman who was granted asylum here from Enemia) will teach Enemian (a language which almost nobody knows in the U.S.). Sister Clare (who is already our Chemistry teacher) will also teach Drama. Una (one of our four Biology teachers) will also teach Art. And I (also on the Biology team) have been asked to teach Music and Choir.

One person missing from our Community is our Professor. My hunch is that he'd like to move in with us, but he lives in a senior housing unit and is afraid of losing his benefits. I'll try to persuade him again later after he gets here. But he better hurry! Una's already looking at her wristwatch, ready to begin.

"Welcome to the 22nd meeting of the Machinists Union" announces a smiling Una at exactly twelve noon.

I'm happy that Una is always so punctual - especially now with our Community and the high school starting up. So much is happening upstairs with the Mendel School and Community that we've got to make sure we don't slack off down here with our monthly meetings. We've got to make sure that those of us living in the Monastery never see ourselves as being 'more committed' or 'more important' than the other Machinists. That would be a Fundamental Attribution Error for sure. The newbies down here are just as committed and just as important as we are. They simply don't have the kinds of lives that allow them to drop everything and join a commune. Some have children and even grandchildren. We have to stay aware of this and never let any 'us/them' divisions form between the new Mendel Community and the old Machinists Union #631.

As if she were reading my mind, Una announces "With so much going on upstairs and with so many new people recently joining us down here, maybe we should get to know each other better. Maybe next month we could meet instead at Tower Grove Park for a picnic."

"Yes!" we all respond.

"Bring your families!" shouts Sister Clare over the hubbub.

"Forget the families - just bring desserts!" shouts a newbie.

B.B. offers to bring one of the Beans & Rice carts. I write a note to myself to reserve a pavilion.

In our meeting today we get off topic and begin fantasizing how differently the 1940's might have turned out had an organized group of Machinists been around.

Our Genocide Slide would have shown us exactly where everything was heading. It would have foreshown the ovens of Auschwitz, the fire-bombing of Tokyo, the carnage at Hiroshima and Nagasaki. The Genocide Slide would have explicitly forbidden us from characterizing the Germans and the Japanese as inhuman.

Our fountain-flushes might have defused the hysteria whipped up at war rallies.

Our Incompat films could have awakened the Europeans to the plight of the Jews. Our Incompat stories could have educated our own citizens about the suffering in Japan.

Although we're a day late and a dollar short, it's fun to speculate how things could have been different. But as our meeting progresses, my mind is wandering. I'm worried about our Professor. He's still not here. He wasn't at the Hiroshima remembrance a couple weeks ago either. It's not like him to miss a meeting. If he doesn't show up in the next hour or so, I'm going out to find him.

33. Monkey See

September is turning out to be a roller coaster of activity and emotion. The lowest point - by far - is our discovery that our Professor has cancer - advanced pancreatic cancer. I found it out when I went looking for him after our August meeting.

At one of our Evening Meetings, I asked the others if we might use one of our extra rooms as a hospice for our Professor.

"Absolutely!" replied B.B. "Michael, you do whatever you need to do to get this done." Not one person objected. In fact they all expressed gratitude and even pride that our Professor would be with us again.

The following Saturday, Zero and I drove to the Senior Center to collect him and his few possessions. Our old teacher was very happy and talked the whole way back. When we got to Mendel, we took the elevator up to the 3rd Floor. When we got to our floor and the elevator doors opened, the whole Community was standing there to welcome him. Holding tightly to his walker, he showed his happiness by dancing a jig for a second or two. We all cheered.

But the celebration didn't last for long. Although he puts on a brave face, our Professor is obviously in a lot of pain. Zero and I were given a bag full of different medications that he needs to take at various times throughout the day. There are opiates to help with the pain, stool softeners and laxatives to manage the side effects of the opiates, plus a smorgasbord of vitamins and other pills. It was confusing, so I made a chart and posted it outside his bathroom door to help us keep things straight.

We moved our only television from the Community Room to our Professor's room so he could watch it from his bed. We take turns looking after him and giving him his medications whenever they are due.

On the third Sunday of September, the whole Machinists Union and our families meet in Tower Grove Park. We're lucky to have so many beautiful parks in St. Louis. This one's very special. Tower Grove Park is a 289-acre Victorian park donated to the people of St. Louis by Henry Shaw, a hardware store owner. It's special for many reasons – one being its botanical diversity. It has hundreds of different kinds of trees and shrubs – more varieties than any other urban park in the country (at least that's what we tell ourselves). We call it a 'Victorian' park because nestled among the trees there are gardens and statues and ornate picnic shelters built during the Victorian era. I was able to reserve one of these historical picnic shelters for our meeting today. It's a large one with the curious name 'Sons of Rest Pavilion'.

(Sons of Rest Pavilion in Tower Grove Park)

A half hour before our meeting, many have already arrived. Una is under the pavilion, setting up a podium. Little Twimfina is wiping off the picnic tables. I'm nearby, crawling in the grass with a magnifying glass and a camera, trying to photograph different weeds. A newbie approaches with a picnic basket and two young children. Twimfina, who doesn't often get to play with those her own age, puts down her washcloth and runs over to meet them.

Coach arrives on his bicycle and shouts when he sees me:

"Hey Michael, what are you doing on the ground with a magnifying glass? Lookin' for your brain?" (I don't know why I find this guy so funny, but I do.)

Soon lots of adults and children are approaching, carrying picnic-baskets and folding-chairs and covered-dishes. Some of our own Mendel Science High students have come, although they're all sticking together. I see B.B. driving across the grass with a Beans & Rice cart.

It's fun to match people with their families. I can tell right away who Daifu's parents are, even though I've never met them before. Una cheerfully greets everybody, points to the food table where they can put their dishes, and then helps them find a place to sit.

As soon as everybody is seated and facing the podium, we can hear the far-away bells from the Church of the Free Will ringing in the distance.

"I hear the bells!" smiles Una. "That means it's 12:00 – time to get started!" (*She waits as the chatter subsides.*) "Welcome to the 23rd meeting of the Machinists Union."

Una doesn't ask me where we left off or discuss any of our usual topics. With so many children and students here, she jumps directly to today's Presentation.

"For today's Presentation, one of our own Biology teachers, Simi, has brought a special guest for us. So I'd like to ask all the children and students to come up here to the front so you can see better." (*There's some commotion as the children come forward, exchanging seats with adults who then move farther back; after a while Una resettles the group*).

"Okay, I think we're ready. Now let's all call out to Simi." (*All of us follow her gentle sing-song example and call 'Simi… Simi… Simi…' Soon Simi appears from the little garden building behind us and walks towards us carrying a baby ape. We all react with 'oohs' and 'ahs'.*)

When Simi arrives under the pavilion, she says: "Do I have a surprise for you! I want to introduce you to my new friend. His name is 'Bo-Bo'. Can you say 'Hello, Bo-Bo'? (*All of us – children and adults – repeat 'Hello, Bo-Bo.'*)

Simi chuckles a little and says: "Bo-Bo's being a little shy now. Does anybody know what Bo-Bo is?" (*Many of the children shout out 'a monkey'; One of the Mendel students shouts out 'a squid'*)

"Monkey? No. Monkeys have tails. But look, Bo-Bo does not have a tail – so Bo-Bo is not a monkey." (*A child calls out 'Chimpanzee'*) "Chimpanzee? Well, you're very, very close. Chimpanzees are apes and Bo-Bo is an ape too. But Bo-Bo is a little smaller than a chimpanzee – and some people think he looks a little more human because his lips have more color – and see how his hair is so nicely parted on the top of his head?" (*"Oh, that's cute!" say some of the children.*) "Yes, that *is* cute!" repeats Simi.

(Simi with Bobo)

Finally a shy child with a half-raised hand timidly asks "a Bonobo?"

"That's right!" exclaims Simi joyfully. "Bo-Bo is a bonobo! Can you all say 'bo-NO-bo'?"

"bo-NO-bo" we all repeat.

"Good! Bonobos are very rare. Most people have never even *seen* one before! There's only one place in the whole world where bonobos live – and that's a beautiful place in the middle of Africa called the Congo. That's where Bo-Bo's home is. That's where his family lives. And the *reason* most people have never seen a bonobo before is because there aren't many bonobos left in the world. Most *zoos* don't even have any – not even our famous St. Louis Zoo where I work. Bo-Bo is just a visitor here. But people who know about bonobos really love them. People love bonobos because they're so peaceful. Instead of fighting with each other, they try to cooperate and make friends. That's why I think Bo-Bo is so noble. Can you say '**Bo-Bo the noble bonobo**'? (*We all try a few times with mixed success; everybody laughs.*)

"Does anybody know why we like to study apes like Bo-Bo? Yes? (*she asks a child with a raised hand*).

"Because we can learn things about ourselves?"

"You're right!" responds Simi. "We can learn a *lot* about ourselves when we learn about Bo-Bo. Who would like to make friends with Bo-Bo and learn about him?" (*The children all wave their hands and plead "Me! Me!"*)

"Well then, Bo-Bo and I will come back after lunch so that you can all get to know him. Are there any last questions about Bo-Bo before we go?"

An adult from the back row asks: Simi, if we were to follow the bonobos backwards in time for millions of years, would they gradually become more and more humanlike?"

"As we went *backwards* in time?" asks Simi.

Another adult warns: "Be careful, Simi, it's a trap!" (*everybody laughs*)

But Simi is un-trappable. "I guess it's possible. We sometimes have the bad habit of thinking that *humans* evolved while the other great apes remained frozen in time. But of course that can't be true. I just don't know the fossil record well enough to answer your question."

Then comes another question from the adults: "Simi, you said that the bonobo communities are gentler than the chimpanzee communities. What would happen if a bonobo were raised in a chimpanzee community?"

Simi chuckles a little. "Did Coach put you up to this?" (*Everybody laughs*.) "When I asked if there were any questions, I was thinking of something like: 'Does Bo-Bo prefer apples or bananas?' (*Everybody laughs again*.)

A little girl raises her hand. "Yes?" asks Simi.

"Does Bo-Bo prefer apples or bananas?" (*Everybody laughs*) "Oh you sweet girl!" exclaims Simi as she steps forward and pats her shoulder with her free hand. "Bananas – just like in the cartoons!"

Then Simi gently takes Bo-Bo's arm and waves it to us. "Say 'bye-bye', Bo-Bo!" We all gently repeat: "Bye-bye, Bo-Bo" as Simi and Bo-Bo leave the pavilion and walk back towards the parking lot.

As they walk away, Una calls out to them: "Thank you, Simi! Thank you, Bo-Bo! See you both after lunch!" Una then turns to us and says: "That's it – time to eat!"

And with that, our feast begins. B.B.Brice and Sister Clare both go to the cart and begin ladling-out bowls of vegetarian chili.

"What *is* this stuff?" says one of the children looking into her bowl. Needless to say, the dessert table was a much bigger hit with the kids.

34. Topsy Turvy

✿

October. In my imagination, I can hear Una saying "Welcome to the 24th meeting of the Machinists Union." But I'm not downstairs with them this month. It's the first time I've ever missed a meeting. I'm staying up here with our Professor because I don't want anybody else seeing him. It's hard to explain why. It's like I want to protect the good memories people have of him.

Medications can change people - can give them different personalities. A lifetime of kindness can be sullied by pills in a medicine bottle. Death is going to claim our bodies, there's no way around it. But it doesn't have to claim our reputations.

Earlier this month our Professor had become very hyper. It was weird. He wandered up and down the halls all day and all night long. He also became very clumsy, knocking over everything. We had to childproof his room. We had to disable the elevator. We had to put plastic sheeting over his windows and over the hall windows so that he wouldn't break them, or worse yet fall through them. We had to keep all our doors locked when we weren't in our rooms lest he come in and innocently destroy everything.

The hospice nurse who visits every few days switched a couple of his pain medications once again so that he wouldn't be so restless. But it only seems to have made him worse.

Yesterday, Saturday, I asked Julie Jean to substitute for me and take care of our Professor while Zero and I went to Badluck Jail. Zero wanted me to visit Dougie-the-druggie with him.

Initially I had no desire to ever associate with Dougie. He had caused way too much pain for B.B. and the rest of us. But later as I thought about it, I remembered that our Professor had specifically talked about this a few months earlier. He had predicted that this would be one of our great defining challenges. Would we see Dougie as an evil person? Or would we be able to look inside and see the gears turning – the wheels and pinions that caused him to do what he did. And if we were indeed able to see the gears, what would we do? Would we jump up on the grand stage and sing in the spotlight like a 'Lawrence Olivier Machinist'? Or would we be an 'Everyday Machinist' and do something practical that really made a difference? I choose the latter, Professor. I choose to be an Everyday Machinist.

So after we had lunch, Zero gave me a ride to Badluck Jail. Zero has been coming to this jail every weekend for years, so quite a few of the guards know him by name. Nevertheless before entering the prison, he has to go through the same security search that I and everybody else have to go through. They open his backpack and take out five dice, a dice cup and a score-pad.

"I see you've got another big Yahtzee game going today, Zero" chuckles a guard. "What's this for?" he asks as he holds up a wood embroidery hoop."

"That's to keep the dice from rolling off the table" answers Zero.

"Oh, good idea!" he exclaims.

A different guard carrying a walkie-talkie escorts us into the prison proper and through a labyrinth of halls and gates. It's a noisy place – a place loud with men's voices. In one hall I can hear an especially loud group of men chanting:

"Bang-Bang-BANG! Look at ME! I gotta gun, I'm a SOMEbody!
Bang-Bang-BANG! Look at ME! I gotta gun, I'm a SOMEbody!"

When we reached the sunroom, Dougie is already seated at the table. A guard is waiting for us at the door. "Have a nice game, gentlemen" she says cheerfully as she opens the door for us.

Dougie is jubilant to see Zero. He shakes his hand like a long lost friend. Zero then introduces me to Dougie.

"I'm so happy to meet you, Michael" he warmly says as he shakes my hand.

The three of us spend a minute or two talking about the weather and the Cardinals' chances of making it to the World Series. Then Zero takes the game pieces out of his backpack.

When I see what is about to happen, I tell them: "I'm sorry, but I never learned how to play Yahtzee. You two play without me."

"No, we want *you* to play too" says Dougie imploringly.

Zero dismisses my plea right away: "Oh, c'mon, Michael – it's simple."

"Great" I think to myself. Now I get to demonstrate to everybody what a slow learner I am. I hate being in this situation – hate having to learn complicated things under pressure. But Dougie picks up a score-pad and explains the game to me slowly and clearly – so slowly and clearly that I get the thrilling feeling that I might actually understand it.

We end-up playing four games. And although I didn't win a single one, I really enjoyed it. I never lost by much because whenever I tried to do something foolish, Dougie would lightly suggest that I think it over again.

As we walk back to the car, I mention to Zero how much I enjoyed the game – and how pleasant it was being with such a sweet man.

He chuckles and replies "Yeah, that happens a lot here. That's why I brought you!"

When we get back to Mendel, I go up to check on our Professor. Before I reach his room, I can hear his angry voice shouting obscenity-laden abuses. When I get there I find Julie with tears in her eyes. Our Professor is writhing in his bed in a hateful stupor. Poor Julie was the only target around. We step out into the hall.

"It's the medicine, it's not you" I tell her.

"I know" she replies. "But it still hurts."

"Can I take over now?" I ask her.

"If you don't mind" she replies. "I changed his diaper about an hour ago. He wasn't so agitated then. But after I gave him his medicine, all of this started."

I thank Julie and then go back into the room. The diaper had come off and feces was smeared all over the sheet and the old man's leg. He then begins crying - crying loudly as only a broken man can cry.

I hold him and try to sooth him by repeating over and over: "We're going to get through this, Professor. We're going to get through this."

What a confusing, topsy-turvy day it has been with a devil

turning into an angel and an angel turning into a devil. But I'm a Machinist and I don't use words like these. I don't even want these words in my head. Still, it happened.

35. Thanksgiving

✿

November. In the news there are often reports of people "dying peacefully in their sleep". It sounds nice – certainly better than "dying in horrible pain". But I tend not to believe it. Especially now.

Our Professor got weaker and weaker. He stopped talking, he stopped moving. He just lay there comatose in his bed. We placed an oxygen tube near his nose to help him breathe.

We all took turns staying with him, talking to him, swabbing his mouth with water, administering the morphine solution every few hours, and holding his hand day and night. He fought hard for each breath, minute after minute, hour after hour. Five days later he was still fighting, but his breathing had grown shallow – so shallow that Sister Clare and I had to lean close just to hear him. He'd gasp and then there'd be silence. Sister Clare and I looked at each other, wondering if it was over – then he'd gasp again. This went on for several more hours. Sometime before dawn he gasped and there was silence. Sister Clare and I looked at each other and wondered if it was over. It was.

There was no funeral, no public visitation. However yesterday, Saturday, the twelve of us had a little remembrance in which we did something both meaningful and practical with his ashes.

The sidewalk slab directly in front of Mendel's front step has long been broken and unlevel. It's a tripping hazard. So we dug out the old slab, and then reverently stirred our Professor's ashes into a reinforced mix of Portland cement, sand and water. After we poured it into the frame, tamped it down and smoothed its surface, Una scratched the words "Every Day" into the setting concrete with large letters. We all then added our thumbprints here and there. Twimfina left her whole handprint.

Today after our Machinists Union meeting, we're having a more proper ceremony. The forty of us have gathered outside on this bracing late November afternoon and have crowded around the new sidewalk slab - which is now as hard as a rock.

We start by retelling memories we have of our Professor, but they soon drift into testimonials.

"Professor, we've learned so many important things from you" says Coach. "From that first day in EP101 to the last, you've been our constant teacher, model and friend."

"Hear, hear!" we shout.

Una concludes by saying: "And so it is with love and gratitude that we the Machinists Union – *your* Machinists Union – dedicate this most important bit of sidewalk to you." She then reaches down, slips off her shoe, and places her bare foot on the cold concrete. "You are the one who led us here. You have always been our stepping-stone, and you always will be. Thank you, Professor."

"Thank you, Professor" we all respond. Many of us also take off a shoe so that we can feel the cold and the warmth of it all. As I extend my bare foot towards the slab, I close my eyes and listen to the others as they do the same. Whispered and shouted, high-pitched and low, I hear "Thank you, Professor" over and over and over.

Later in the afternoon after the Machinists Union had gone home, Una, Coach, Zero, Sister Clare and I are in the Beans & Rice kitchen, cleaning sacks of raw beans.

"Man, look at all the dirt and rocks I'm finding in these pinto beans" whines Una.

Coach replies "Just throw them in that trash can over there. Oops, I'm sorry, that's one of your hats." We all laugh.

"Have you noticed that we five are together again?" asks Sister Clare. "It's kind of nice, isn't it? We've always had a good chemistry together."

Yes, we've got that certain *je ne sais quoi*" says Zero with an exaggerated French pronunciation. Una rolls her eyes.

"Now we can have that orgy we've always wanted" says Coach.

"Great idea! You go first, big guy!" replies Sister Clare. Everybody laughs.

"Well surprise, surprise" begins Una in her sarcastic voice. Here we are, all college graduates - except for Michael of course -

and what are we doing? We're cleaning beans. What a bunch of losers."

"Hey, we don't use that word around here" I quip.

"Then why's it stamped on your forehead?" she returns. Everybody laughs.

Twimfina comes skipping into the kitchen to join us.

"Hey you, get to work!" growls Coach with feigned bossiness.

"No child labor" Twimfina informs him. We all laugh. I think to myself: "Someday this five-year-old is going to be a force to reckon with."

"I heard Corky's out of jail and has a new job" says Zero.

"Good for him. He deserves it" says Sister Clare.

"We can probably assume that *everybody* from EP101 has a job by now - a good, high-paying biotech job" whines Una. "And here we are sorting beans. Now why is that?"

"Because our lives just happened to take us into a classroom taught by a certain Professor" I answer. (There's a long pause of silence.)

"Well, aren't we the lucky ones" says Sister Clare. (There's a smidgin of real happiness in our resigned chuckles.)

"Yes, aren't we the lucky ones" repeats Twimfina.

Afterword

The story you've just read is fictional. I wish it were true, but it's not. However it *could* be, couldn't it? There *could be* a community that follows an Ethics of Luck. There *could be* a community of active pacifists who use their tools to defuse social hatreds.

If this '*could be*' community is to ever become real, some real person is going to have to start it. Maybe you? Might you be the person to start a Machinists Union #554 in Minneapolis, or a Machinists Union #871 in Albuquerque? There are lots of determinists, lots of cities, and lots of zip-code prefixes!

There's a sequel to "*Aren't We the Lucky Ones*". It's a musical play titled "Twimfina". It follows the life of Una's daughter Twimfina into adulthood. Although I never mentioned it in "*Aren't We the Lucky Ones*", the name "Twimfina" is an acronym for "The World Is My Family, I'm Not Afraid. Having been raised in the Mendel Community under an Ethics of Luck, she's a force of nature. The musical is scored for piano and singers - lots and lots of singers of all ages. I've put it in the public domain and online for free download. Please take a chance with it.

Thanks for reading "Aren't We The Lucky Ones". I always appreciate any suggestions for improving it.

- Secretary Michael
twimfina@gmail.com

Social disasters don't suddenly appear out of nowhere.
They develop step-by-step.
The Genocide Slide is a tool used to measure these steps.

Genocide Slide
— Four Steps Down into Social Disaster —

Step 1: *Unnecessary Grouping*

The first step down the Genocide Slide occurs when people are grouped together. People are commonly grouped together in many ways – by age, by occupation, by ethnicity, by blood type, by income, by anything. Although grouping can be useful, it is also the **necessary first step** to something horrible. All grouping creates division – division between "members" and "non-members", between the "in's" and the "out's", between the "we's" and the "they's".

VIOLATORS: We violate *Step 1* when we unnecessarily group people together or cause another person to *feel* unwantedly grouped. We also violate *Step 1* when we support organizations that are not diverse.

OBLIGATION: It is our obligation to avoid unnecessary grouping. It is our obligation to avoid using words that unnecessarily identify groups. And when physical differences are apparent, it is our obligation to support and practice diversity. It is our obligation to keep ourselves and our children totally off the Genocide Slide – far away at *"Step Zero"* where the world is an ungrouped family.

Step 2: _Avoidance_ (Jokes, Stereotyping, Negative Speech)

The second step down the Genocide Slide occurs when people of any group are avoided or spoken of in a negative way. This includes jokes. Joking and making negative comments about a group creates hard-to-erase stereotypes. Avoidance of others is unhealthy because it perpetuates ignorance. It's mixing and open communication that keeps a person and a society healthy.

VIOLATORS: We violate _Step 2_ when we avoid people who are different from us, when we joke about them, when we speak poorly of them, or when we cause them to _feel_ that we are doing these things.

OBLIGATION: It is our obligation to never laugh at or show approval of a demeaning joke or comment about a group. It is our obligation to openly mix and communicate with people from other groups to prevent stereotypes from taking hold.

Step 3: _Hate Speech_ (Dehumanization, Denial of Equal Access)

The third step down the Genocide Slide occurs when disgust or hatred is expressed towards a group, when they are referred to in nonhuman terms (such as "insects" or "enemies") or when they are denied access to the same fruits of society that others enjoy.

VIOLATORS: We violate _Step 3_ when we express disgust or hatred towards another group, or when we refer to them in non-human terms, or when we allow social doors to close on them, or when we cause them to _feel_ that we are doing these things.

OBLIGATION: When we observe any _Step 3_ hatred, we have an obligation to counteract the violation, immediately and publicly, so that those who hear the hate can be empowered by its rejection. It is our challenge to do this in a way that will heal and free (instead of harden and trap) the violator. It is the job of our schools to teach students how to rebuke _Step 3_ violators effectively but kindly.

Step 4: *Causing Fear or Harm*

People who engage in or incite physical attacks against those they perceive to be in another group must be quarantined from society until they are no longer consumed with such hatred. Like viruses, hatred spreads and infects others. The contagion must be stopped.

VIOLATORS: We violate *Step 4* when we directly or indirectly endanger the safety or well-being of someone in another group, or when they *feel* endangered as a result of our actions or lack of action.

OBLIGATION: It is our obligation to stand up like a wall and block all violence and all incitement to violence. If the police and court system are the most effective way to achieve this, it is our obligation to contact the police and to testify in court until the targeted group is safe and the attacker is confined and given the chance to grow in a different direction.

"People who are aware of, and ashamed of, their prejudices are well on the road to eliminating them."

-Gordon Allport

B.B.Brice Recipes

Several bean and rice dishes were mentioned in the book. Having prepared these vegetarian dishes hundreds of times, I'll 'spill the beans' on everything I know about cooking them. But first and more importantly, here are a few observations about preparing beans in general:

1. INSPECT THE BEANS
It's surprising how many rocks and chunks of dirt can be found in a bag of beans. Some types of beans, like split peas, almost never have impurities. But others, like pinto beans, can have plenty.

I inspect them by opening the top of the bag and then slowly sprinkling them into my hand as I look at them carefully under adequate lighting. When my hand is full, I empty it into a container and then start with my next handful. I imagine that sprinkling the beans onto a white tray might be a good way to do it too.

2. WASH THE BEANS
Fill the container of beans with water and swish it around. Even though the beans may look clean, the water often becomes cloudy. If so, empty the water from the container (a strainer makes it easier) and refill with water again to rewash. (Black turtle beans keep leaching an ink into the wash water. That's okay - it's not dirt.)

I don't rinse split peas more than once, even though the water is always cloudy. I figure that they were protected in their pod so there should be no dirt on them. Plus I feel it's a bit wasteful to wash the split peas much because they seems to disintegrate in the water, turning the water green. Another trick they do when they get wet is to cling to their neighbors like little vacuum cleaners. They'll form a big cannonball that'll splash when you try to empty them into a pan. Some will also cling to the container and have to be slid off by hand.

3. SOAK THE BEANS

You have to be organized to have beans in your diet. They're not a "I think I'll whip up some beans for lunch" type of food. The dry beans will first have to be soaked (unless you're preparing split peas or lentils). When beans are soaked they absorb water and almost triple in volume. After you've done it a few times, you'll be able to judge whether they've soaked long enough by how high they've risen in the soaking container. Four hours should probably be long enough. However soaking them overnight never fails.

When the soaking is over, I always throw away the soaking water and rinse them. I never use the soaking water to cook the beans. Why? It's my understanding that a water-soluble sugar (oligosaccharide) is leached into the water during soaking. This sugar is difficult for our bodies to digest, causing gas. Beans already have a bad reputation for causing gas in some people. This seems like an easy way to reduce that problem.

4. COOK THE BEANS

I *always* use a pressure cooker. I love soft beans. The softer the better. The best chance of getting soft beans is to cook them in water alone. Only after they're melt-in-the-mouth soft would I ever add another ingredient. I hear it's especially important to not add acids (like tomato or lemon) until after the beans are soft - or else they'll *never* get soft! Disliking hard beans as I do, I never risked checking out this claim with an experiment.

How much water should be used to cook beans? There are lots of variables, such as the cooking temperature used, the kind of pan used (some pans lose more water through evaporation than others), the length of time cooked, and the type of bean cooked (lentils and split peas usually aren't pre-soaked, so they'll absorb more water during cooking than will the pre-soaked beans). So it's best to experiment and keep notes.

Even though I use a pressure cooker, I cook them a long time - usually an hour or more. I have such a fear of hard beans that I take no chances. In my opinion, you can't overcook beans.

I've heard conflicting information about the effect of salt on bean softness. Since I haven't used salt (or fat) for many years in my bean dishes, I've no personal experience to share.

Sometimes the beans just won't get soft even if you soak them for a week and use a nuclear-powered pressure cooker. This is probably caused by age. I don't know how old is 'too old'. Storage conditions are probably a factor. But I've often cooked old beans with no problem. (In fact I just finished the last of my 100 bags of black beans that I bought a few years back when they went on sale for 47 cents each at Shop & Save.) On the rare occasions when my beans don't get melt-in-your-mouth soft, I put them in a blender and liquefy them. It's quite delicious. 'Gazpacho' is the proper name for cold liquefied bean soup. However drinking your beans (or any food for that matter) from a cup really pours on the calories fast!

As far as I know, eating beans regularly is very nutritious. I always feel good after eating beans. It's rare that I have a day without them. It's also inexpensive and very fast (because I prepare a large pot of beans once or twice a week, store it in the refrigerator, and then simply put a portion in the microwave whenever I'm hungry.)

RICE: Although bean dishes are certainly fine alone, rice is a good companion for them. I understand that there's a nutritional advantage to having both in our diet. Beans are said to provide the essential amino acid lycine that is absent in rice, and rice is said to be rich in several essential amino acids that beans are poor in. And so the two foods complement each other so that our bodies can make complete proteins.

Rice cookers are magical. You just throw in the rice and water and walk away. Although pure brown rice is fine, I usually have a container of different grains that I've mixed together: brown rice, sweet rice, barley, wild rice, millet. White rice is the same as brown rice, except that the nutritious outer coating has been ground away. (That's the reason I don't buy white rice, delicious and fluffy as it is.) It's too bad they've recently discovered arsenic in rice. It's curbed my enthusiasm for it a little. I bought a bread machine.

BEANS: Dry beans are sold here in 1-pound or 2-pound bags. Since I use a large 8-quart pressure cooker (Presto 1370), I usually prepare two pounds at once. It saves time and heat energy.

I've always mentally grouped beans into different categories, not knowing exactly why. I was happy to discover that the categories make botanical sense because each category represents a different species (and sometimes even a different genus) from the others.

1. COMMON (pinto, black, cranberry, red, pink, yellow, white, kidney, etc.). To my undeveloped palate, all these wonderful beans taste pretty-much the same and can be used interchangeably. The kidneys might be a little firmer than the others and the yellow mayocobas might be a little creamier than the others, but they're close enough. I usually choose black beans (which are often the cheapest too!)
[Botanical name: Phaseolus vulgaris]

2. LIMA BEANS
Our stores carry both the large beans and the baby beans. I think they're actually different cultivars, not different maturity stages of the same bean. I like them both and usually buy whichever type is on sale. They really swell up huge during soaking.
[Botanical name: Phaseolus lunatus]

3. LENTILS
These wonderful little lenses don't need to be soaked before cooking (although I've read that if you soak them long enough to sprout, they're even more nutritious.) I always buy the brown ones with the husk still on. I feel that eating the green ones that look like split peas or the red or pink ones is like eating white rice. I've heard that they have a different flavor, but I'll probably never know. Lentils are a staple in India. I like them soft as oatmeal and in a tomato base. I prepare lots of lentils. In winter I bake a vegetarian meatloaf using lentils smooshed together with ingredients such as sweet potatoes, rolled oats, tomato paste and different spices (but no salt or fat of course!)
[Botanical name: Lens culinaris]

4. SPLIT PEAS

There's nothing like a hearty bowl of split pea soup on a cold winter's day! Although green split peas seem to be more common, yellow split peas are also available. (Remember that Gregor Mendel counted both colors in his experiments!) I've read that the yellow ones are milder, but I've not noticed that myself. I just stick with the green ones. (Note: You have to be careful using a pressure cooker with split peas because they can clog the vent. We have indelible green stains on our kitchen ceiling to prove it!)
[Botanical name: Pisum sativum]

OTHER GREAT BEAN SPECIES:
There are other bean categories that weren't mentioned as being on the 'B.B.Brice - Beans & Rice' menu. Hopefully someday they will be.

CHICKPEAS (GARBANZOS): People all over the world depend on this famous bean. I used to think they were called 'chick' peas because the bean looks like the face of a baby chicken, with a cute little beak sticking out. Recently I found out that the etymology of the name has nothing to do with chicks or chickens. When I cook these I often use curry powder.
[Botanical name: Cicer arietinum]

BLACK-EYED PEAS: Well, they're pretty. I know they're famous in the South. However they have a very distinctive flavor that I haven't yet come to appreciate.
[Botanical name: Vigna unguiculata]

FAVA BEANS (BROAD BEANS): The beans are huge. I cooked a few but was disappointed. It's another bean with a distinctive flavor that I'm not fond of yet. Plus each bean has a tough skin that has to be peeled off. It takes forever. So I gave up and just went out into the garden and planted the rest of the bag. Not long after that dozens of fava bean plants started popping up! They aren't climbers like other bean plants. They're tall, sturdy, upright, self-supporting plants. They have beautiful blossoms with deep black spots on them. From the blossoms grew green pods with those big beans inside. But these beans were delicious! They were mild and meaty and very tender. And they didn't have a tough skin that had to be peeled off! Even the pod was very sweet and tender! So there's a world of difference between dried fava beans and fresh fava beans!

[Botanical name: Vicia faba]

Here are the five salt-free, fat-free vegetarian bean dishes mentioned in the book with a few words about each:

VEGETARIAN CHILI: any of the common beans will work; pinto and kidney beans together seem appropriate; a tomato base is essential; cumin gives it that distinctive flavor, and also hungarian paprika to a lesser extent; I used to add TVP (textured vegetable protein) made from soy to give it "meat", but it contains salt so I stopped. I add chopped onion after the beans have cooked to give it some crunch.

RED BEAN TANGERINE: a traditional Chinese dish which uses the Chinese adzuki bean, along with sugar, lotus seeds and tangerine skin. The adzuki bean *[Botanical name: Vigna angularis]* has a black-eyed pea flavor that I'm not yet crazy about;

CELERY SPLIT PEA: traditionally mint and carrots are added to split pea soup, however I use parsnips for sweetness, chopped celery for crunch, and black pepper for spice;

LEMON LIMAS: either the large or baby lima beans will work; an important ingredient is dried lime (also called lemon omani); fennel seed adds a sweet licorice flavor and acts as a carminative; other appropriate spices include coriander seed, tarragon and black pepper; add corn for 'Lemon Lima Succotash';

POTATO-TOMATO LENTILS: I used to cook the potatoes with the lentils, but burned them to the bottom of the pot so many times that I now always cook them separately; curry spices go well with this dish;

Index of Concepts

Acceptance of Multiple Truths

 Lasagna Lesson 58

Active Pacifism

 Against Guns, Disgunsemble................................ 107, 109
 Against Violent Films.................................... 86
 Against War (Peace Vigil) 77
 Radio Metaphor 75
 Unfairness of Violence 65
 Work of Machinists, Active not Passive 68

Animal Oneness

 Bobo the Bonobo 148
 'One Health' Presentation.............................. 95

Behavior Change

 'Brains Controlled by Bugs' Presentation 138
 Corky's Tumor 56
 Professor's Medications................................ 150
 Psychopathy, ASPD...................................... 66

Blameworthiness

 Insight from Determinism 42

Candelescence

 Definition 124

Community

 Defined.. 116

Danger of Grouping

Coach's Argument against 'Teams' 135
Step One of Genocide Slide 160

Determinism

Billiard Analogy 18
Keeping Distance (Sun, Plumbing, Flashlight Analogies)......... 39, 41
Neuroscience 'Proof' (Libet Study) 72

Ethics of Luck

Gold Standard, Book Metaphor 65
Protecting the Unlucky from the Scourge of the Lucky 62

Fountain-Flush

At Badluck Jail 129
At Doofus Gunshop.. 108
At Testosterone Theater 88
Defined.. 83

Fundamental Attribution Error

Definition 48
Doctor Frank 106

Genocide Slide

Entire Document in Appendix... 160
Inception 77
Used to Analyze Film.. 86

Incompat

Definition 138

Instability from Deterministic Thoughts

Group as Beacon of Hope 35
Michael's Account of Instability.. 19
Pastor Causasui's Condemnation of Suicide 29
Talking Lauterkeit out of Danger.. 139

Power Corrupts

In Zero's Valedictorian Speech 9

Prison Reform

Badluck Jail Fountain-Flush 129
Chance to Live Decent Lives 42
Prison as Healing 128
Stanford Prison Experiment 128

Tools to Change People without Violence

Fountain-Flushes 83
How the Tools Could Have Changed History 143
Incompat Films and Art.. 138
Peaceful Demonstrations / Vigils 77
Teaching 123

Vocabulary

Purging of Words Incompatible with Determinism 45

Wealth

Candelescence 124
Doctor Frank 101

www.ingramcontent.com/pod-product-compliance
Lightning Source LLC
Chambersburg PA
CBHW050946030426
42339CB00007B/315